'The Faithworks Campaign has d[...]
political parties. The practical help [...]
charities to some of Britain's most vulnerable people and com[...]
transforming lives in ways often unmatched by secular alternatives.
Government needs to work in closer partnership with faith-based and
other community initiatives that are rescuing lives from poverty, addic-
tion and alienation. Faithworks Unpacked *challenges Britain's
churches to increase the effectiveness of existing projects and to explore
starting new projects too. It could not be more timely.'*

Rt Hon. Iain Duncan Smith MP
Conservative Party Leader and Leader of the Opposition

'Faithworks Unpacked *will help church members serve God and our
fellows better – which means more effectively, more intelligently and
professionally. Faith is often better demonstrated by deeds rather than
words. Here is good informed instruction by people who know how.'*

Simon Hughes, Liberal Democrat Shadow Home Secretary
and MP for North Southwark and Bermondsey

'I commend Faithworks *because it is a positive challenge to put truth
into action. There is no limit to the good we can do.'*

J. John, the Philo Trust

'In many churches there is a growing desire to demonstrate the love of
Christ by getting more involved in the diverse needs of their communities. This is a comprehensive and practical resource which addresses
that desire, recognises the wide spectrum of need and motivates us to
fulfil our calling.'*

Nicky Gumbel, Alpha & Holy Trinity Brompton

'The churches have a strong track record of serving local communities. Faithworks Unpacked provides comprehensive and accessible advice to enable us to build on this impressive tradition.'

Sarah Lindsell, Director, Catholic Agency for Social Concern

'A toolkit for every church that wants to roll up its sleeves and get involved in its community big time.'

Andy Hawthorne, Founding Director of the Message Trust

Faithworks Unpacked

STEVE CHALKE

KINGSWAY PUBLICATIONS
EASTBOURNE

ISBN 1 84291 028 0

Published by
KINGSWAY COMMUNICATIONS LTD
Lottbridge Drove, Eastbourne, BN23 6NT, England.
Email: books@kingsway.co.uk

Book design and production for the publishers by
Bookprint Creative Services, P.O. Box 827, BN21 3YJ, England.
Printed in Great Britain.

Contents

Contributors 8
Foreword 10

SECTION 1: Why a Faithworks Movement? 13
1.1: Faithworks: The Task of the Church 15
1.2: The Faithworks Movement 21
1.3: The Faithworks Charter 25
1.4: Faithworks Unpacked 31

SECTION 2: Getting Your Church Involved 33
2.1: Communicating the Vision 35

SECTION 3: Researching Your Community 41
3.1: Why Research? 43
3.2: Where to Begin 45
3.3: Gathering Information 48
3.4: 'Soft' Research Tools 51
   (a) Questionnaires 51
   (b) Interviews 57
   (c) Participatory appraisal methods 60

	(d) Focus groups	61
3.5:	A Five-step Research Plan	64
3.6:	Analysing Your Data	66

SECTION 4: Developing Your Strategy 71

4.1:	Why Plan?	73
4.2:	The Project Team	76
4.3:	The Strategy Wheel	78
	(a) Step 1: Where are we?	79
	(b) Step 2: Where do we want to go?	80
	(c) Step 3: What direction do we take?	82
	(d) Step 4: How are we going to get there?	83
	(e) Step 5: Who is responsible?	84
	(f) Step 6: How are we doing?	84
4.4:	Keeping Records	87
4.5:	Why Evaluate?	96
4.6:	Financial Planning	102
4.7:	Business Plans	115

SECTION 5: How to Implement Your Project 121

5.1:	Forming a Management Committee	123
5.2:	Identifying Potential Funders	126
5.3:	Setting up a Charity	133
5.4:	Building a Team: How to Be Distinctively Christian	151
5.5:	Structuring Your Team	157
5.6:	Working with Volunteers	161
5.7:	Recruiting Staff	168
5.8:	Equal Opportunities and Recruiting Christians	179
5.9:	Employing Staff	189
5.10:	Working with National Government	199
	(a) The Role of MPs	199

(b) Government ministries and departments 202
(c) Regional government 206
5.11: Working with Local Government 209
(a) Local Strategic Partnerships and
Community Strategies 209
(b) 'Best Value' and contracting out 212
(c) Regeneration partnerships 213
(d) Local Government Association best
practice guidelines 215
(e) Contacting your local council and
public agencies 217

**SECTION 6: Faithworks Consultancy,
Membership and Partners 225**
6.1: The Faithworks Consultancy 227
6.2: Becoming a Faithworks Member 229
6.3: The Faithworks Partners 232

SECTION 7: Signing the Charter 247
7.1: Signing the Faithworks Charter 249

Contributors

Although this manual bears my name, it is in fact the result of a huge team effort. My deep thanks, therefore, go to all those who have worked so long and so hard to put together what I believe is the unique resource you have in front of you. I particularly want to thank those who have contributed their time, expertise and professional experience in helping write the various sections.

Joy Madeiros has been Director of Human Resources and Organisation Development for the YMCA for the last ten years. Previously she was a personnel manager and employee relations adviser in the commercial sector.

Penny Baker has worked for many years in the voluntary sector and has experience of supporting scores of small or emerging community projects. She is currently a development officer, helping pilot a national standard for organisations' work with volunteers.

Libby Ferguson was called to the Bar in 1992 and practised as a barrister in the Temple for eight years, before joining an American law firm in the City of London. She has consulted on a variety of charitable projects for the Oasis Trust.

Ed Cox is Research & Liaison Officer with Community Pride Initiative and a minister in the United Reformed Church. Community Pride was established by the mainstream churches in Manchester and Salford working with Church Action on Poverty.

Aredi Pitsiaeli is Development Manager at Oasis Trust. She has many years' experience as a professional project planner and manager.

Alan Mann works for the Oasis Trust as my co-writer. He has an MA in Theology.

My thanks also go to my colleagues at Oasis – Hannah Cavaghan, Nathan Oley, Paul Rodgers, James Griffin, Jonathan Dutton, Dave Hitchcock, Fiona Smith and Sue Fifield, as well as Sarah Lindsell, for the time and energy they have put into checking, advising and editing various aspects of the content.

Steve Chalke

Foreword by the Rt Hon. Paul Boateng MP

There is a balm in Gilead that heals the sin sick soul.
There is a balm in Gilead that makes the shattered whole.

(Nineteenth-century negro spiritual)

Our religion, our faith and its services are empty without the imperative to action that requires us to address the consequences, not least in the field of social policy, of a divided and fragmented world. The love of God and faith in him demands that we as the church formulate a response to the needs of the wider world grappling with poverty, disease, inequality and oppression. This is part of a tradition that goes back to the Old Testament prophets and was handed down to us by Jesus himself, who set out our agenda for us at the beginning of his own ministry in this way:

'The Spirit of the Lord is on me, because he has anointed me to preach good news to the poor. He has sent me to proclaim freedom for the prisoners and recovery of sight for the blind, to release the oppressed, to proclaim the year of the Lord's favour.' (Luke 4:18–19)

This Spirit moved the abolitionists to defeat the slave trade, the great social reformers of the Victorian period to take on the mill owners and the unacceptable face of the Industrial Revolution, challenged segregation in the US and Apartheid in South Africa, caused Christians in Poland and Eastern Europe to range themselves alongside the movement for democratic reform, and most recently has led to church-based and other groups to come together to campaign in Jubilee 2000 to remove the burden of debt from the developing world.

Political parties and institutions cannot ignore these manifestations of the Spirit; indeed they are often themselves influenced in their values by a tradition that has been profoundly affected by church and chapel. The Labour Party, as the late John Smith often pointed out, has always owed more to Methodism than to Marxism. And in government we have, inspired by John's leadership while in Opposition, sought to ensure that the partnerships we are creating with the voluntary and private sector to regenerate and revitalise civil society and the communities in which we live, include and recognise the vital role of faith groups.

This is in no sense to seek to co-opt religion – that would be self-defeating – but rather to recognise not just that the State on its own cannot change the way things are for the better, but that there is the need for real partnership if we are to achieve the vital added value that comes from engagement with faith-based communities. The State has an obvious and major role to play in delivering resources and mobilising effort. But faith-based groups and the voluntary sector bring with them an independence and a closeness to the realities of everyday lives and experience that are invaluable.

If the church is to act to address the needs of the times and to deliver on the imperatives that Christ has called upon us as his followers to witness, we need to equip ourselves for this purpose. This applies equally whether we act on our own or in partnership with others. We cannot hope to create the structures and mechanisms to make a difference to people's lives by ignoring the practicalities of effective organisation and management. The churches need to master these skills, to make them the servants of those in most need; to ensure that, as churches, they have a clear understanding of how best to develop working relationships with other institutions to better deliver that which the churches are uniquely well placed to contribute.

The great asset of the churches is faith itself and a belief in the power of the Holy Spirit to transform the lives of individuals and through them the very nature of the institutions of which they are a part. We are required to provide for the Holy Spirit a channel for his redemptive work, namely our own words and deeds in this world. The cross, an instrument of torture, degradation and death, was transformed by the power of God into a symbol and instrument of liberation and life. Our own imperfect hearts, minds and talents must similarly be transformed into instruments which are capable of working compassion, love and justice in the world.

And the focus of this Christ-like activity can often be the local churches where we meet and worship. It is in and through the body of Christ in the local community that we can and must begin to make real in our communal life and in the lives of our neighbours what we believe about God and what we preach about the way things could be. The church itself then must embrace an agenda of reform and modernisation that is evidence based and analytical, but fired by God's love. This manual is both these things. I commend it wholeheartedly in the spirit of St Augustine, who reminds us: 'hope has two beautiful daughters. Their names are Anger and Courage. Anger at the way things are and Courage to see that they do not remain the way they are.' This is the real challenge of Faithworks – to move from sentiment to strategy.

Rt Hon Paul Boateng MP
Financial Secretary to HM Treasury

SECTION 1:

Why a Faithworks Movement?

1.1: Faithworks: The Task of the Church

The task of the church is simply this: to reflect God, and in doing so demonstrate a faith that works!

Some years ago, on the opening of the Oasis Health Centre, which offers primary health care to many of central London's homeless population, a reporter from a well-known commercial radio station enquired rather accusingly, 'As a Christian charity, aren't you using this as an opportunity to prey on vulnerable and needy homeless people – in reality, opening a centre for proselytism rather than health?' I was able to assure her with complete honesty, 'Our motivation is simply our God-given responsibility to care – our faith must work! If through our work the people we serve encounter God and something of the love and compassion of Jesus then that will speak for itself. We don't hide our faith, but we will never impose it. We are here to serve all, unconditionally. That is what Christ has asked us to do. It's what our faith compels us to do.'

God is subtle

God is love. And this apex of biblical insight necessitates his greatest gift to us: our freedom to choose. Freedom is something we cherish above all things; it is at the very core of what it is to be human. True love always grants freedom. That is why God adopts a subtle approach with us. He leaves us space to make our own decisions and choices. He never pushes, forces, bludgeons, beats, coerces, cajoles, manhandles or manipulates people into faith – he never threatens them with the kind of offer they can't refuse. And Jesus gently wooed people too. His relationship with those he encountered was characterised by what Philip Yancey calls 'the slow, steady undertow of grace'. If God imposed himself on us we would be justified in claiming that he had radically undermined the very freedom he has imparted to us.

It is essential the church takes on board this fundamental biblical principle as we work in the arena of welfare provision. In serving others we demonstrate God's love, and we always leave them the freedom to respond to that love as they choose. Like God we are called to love in action with no strings attached.

God is involved

God is involved. He has not abandoned the world; instead he chooses to engage with us. Redemptive love is prepared to get its hands dirty in an 'alien' environment where its principles may be derided and its vision misunderstood, but where it is most needed and where it will have the most impact. God is not a spectator but a player. And once again he calls his church to live by the same principle. The Old Testament prophet, Micah, reflected the message of his peers such as Isaiah and Amos when he wrote: 'The Lord God has told us what is right and what he demands: "See that justice is done, let mercy be your first concern and humbly obey your God"' (Micah 6:8). This is the theme that Jesus clearly picks up when he addresses the people in the synagogue of his home town, this time using the words of Isaiah, as recorded in Luke 4. Jesus announces that his work is not solely concerned with people's spiritual well-being, but with every dimension of their lives. Too often, in our eagerness to 'preach the gospel', we have forgotten to look back and see the model Jesus left us: a model of compassionate involvement in the needs of communities and individuals at every level.

From social action to social justice

'Your God has had plenty to say to the church in the last few decades, but very little, if anything at all, to say to the nation as a whole,' commented an agnostic contact of mine from one of the national broadsheets. 'He's got a serious case of verbal diarrhoea when it comes to his chosen flock, but when faced with the rest of society he's been struck dumb. He's lost his nerve or lost his interest, or both.' Where has the public, social dimension of prophecy gone? The church has privatised prophecy, leaving a 'nice' God saying 'nice' things to 'nice' people. It's high time the church regained its prophetic edge.

For most churches the long struggle to reconcile social action to the gospel has finally been resolved, but now there is a new challenge: to reconcile social justice to the gospel or, in other words, to reconnect the problems with their causes. While it may be true that the church is called to mirror the Samaritan and carry its injured neighbour (Luke 10:25–37), we have an equal responsibility to ensure that the underlying issues that lead to such injuries are also dealt with. To put it simply, authentically biblical faith calls us to address the system that causes the symptoms. It's time for the church to work for social justice; it's time for the church to get political!

The danger of dualism

The Bible flatly contradicts any idea of a sacred/secular divide. As Former Archbishop of Cape Town, Desmond Tutu, observed, 'If we are to say that religion cannot be concerned with politics, then we are really saying that there is a substantial part of human life in which God's will does not run. If it is not God's, then whose is it?'

The real problem our society faces isn't so much secular-isation as sacralisation on the part of the church – the removal of Christian involvement, influence and truth from mainstream debate. Unless we grasp that it is God's intention to bring the whole of creation back to himself, we will always have a tendency to view the gospel as simply having some social spin-offs or by-product implications for the community, and this will inevitably mean that we end up simply dabbling in community affairs. We may talk a good talk from our own corner, but the fight takes place in the centre of the ring, and that is where the church increasingly needs to be.

More than words

The beginning of John's Gospel famously declares that the Word became flesh. The love, justice and mercy that God demonstrates throughout the Old Testament takes on flesh and blood reality. And the challenge of Jesus to his followers before his ascension was that his work of incarnation be taken on by the church. The sending of the Holy Spirit not only continued the presence of Christ in the church but also empowered that same church to be the presence of God in the world.

Incarnation is for an 'alien' world. It is about vulnerability and genuine engagement. It is about surrendering power and control. It is about leaving the place of safety, stepping out of the comfort zone where we are known and understood, and heading for the remote, risk-filled but needy outpost (Philippians 2:1ff). The incarnation demands, therefore, that we engage beyond our comfort zones, beyond the limits of our control. Our commitment to the doctrine of the incarnation means that we should have a responsibility to get involved, not only with what the church is doing but also with what others are doing. Incarnation requires that we 'play away from home'. We cannot keep ourselves to ourselves. Incarnation necessitates that we serve as school governors and local councillors; it requires that we engage in partnership with local councils, statutory agencies and other voluntary bodies, and work with secular community groups at every level.

No area of life is outside the remit of the church or beyond our God-given responsibility. Does God have nothing to say on education, the environment, poverty, crime, racism, working conditions, immigration, taxation, health?

To be silent on any of these issues is to deny God his rightful place in society. But more than that, it is to deny those affected by these issues the hope of his justice and to rob ourselves of a huge opportunity.

It's time to engage. It's time to demonstrate that our faith works.

1.2: The Faithworks Movement

The Faithworks Movement exists:

1. to empower and inspire every local church to rediscover its role at the hub of the community;
2. to challenge and change the public perception of the church by engaging with both media and government;
3. to promote Christian values within our society.

As the social commentators and historians look back on the first few years of the third millennium, whatever else they have to say they will recall and record that these were the years of the painful reinvention of public services here in the UK.

In every community, rural, suburban and urban, there is the aching need for a fresh approach to tackling besetting needs. The door of opportunity is wide open for every local church with an appetite to get involved. And what's more, the church, which for so long was regarded as the Cinderella of community development, has very clearly been invited to the ball. The only question that remains to be answered is will we have the courage to accept that invitation?

Seize the moment

The Faithworks Movement is a concept whose time has come. The current political climate has opened up an opportunity like never before for the church to work in its rightful place at the heart of every local community. But it is not a time for complacency. As some in government waver, and the battle for the place of faith in the public square goes on, we must demonstrate once again that faith does work and that the church is increasingly a major provider of high quality social welfare that will benefit communities the length and breadth of our nation.

This period of transition in the arena of public services demands that the church seize the moment to stand up and be counted among the key players in local community redevelopment before the opportunity disappears. But we will only be able to do so as we provide social action initiatives in a relevant and thoroughly professional manner. That's what this manual is designed to help you achieve.

It's time to rediscover our roots

The church's roots in welfare provision are deep. In the Old Testament God constantly declares that his people are to 'remember the orphan, the widow and the refugee'. In the New Testament, Peter, Paul and other prominent leaders recognised that churches must be, first and foremost, communities that care. So it was that with such a heritage the church in Britain became the original caring professional, pioneering welfare before there even were any 'secular institutions'. In the Middle Ages it was the churches and monasteries which offered help for those who fell through the cracks in society. And when the upheavals of the eighteenth-century Industrial Revolution destroyed, in just a few generations, a traditional way of life (and welfare) that had existed for hundreds of years, the church was at the forefront of attempts to stem the growing tide of poverty and outright destitution. In fact it was only in the mid-nineteenth century that the government and statutory organisations began to think of themselves as having any significant role to play in welfare provision, and not until the second half of the twentieth century that some politicians began to think the state should have an exclusive one.

The media often write off the local church, claiming it no longer has a role to play or a voice to be heard in our society. But they have got their facts wrong. As our politicians struggle with the huge issues of how to reinvent our social infrastructure, the church has an indispensable role to play. Not simply because our faith motivates us to serve in a sustained, rooted, imaginative and committed way, but because the deepest needs we face are spiritual as well as physical. As Joel Edwards, General Director of the Evangelical Alliance, observed, 'Rumours about the church's untimely death have been rumbling around influential places for a long time. Faithworks is an exciting opportunity to put such rumours to rest.'

However, the Faithworks Movement is not some trendy reinvention of the church. It is the *rediscovery* of the church's roots – a return to its original calling and a demonstration that when it comes to welfare provision, local churches and Christian charities offer rooted, sustainable, committed, imaginative and transforming solutions to the deepest needs of the UK's communities.

One voice, one nation

But to make a real impact in our nation, we have to learn to stand and speak together with one voice. Now is the time to address the government's agenda and to work with government to explore practical ways in which the church can play its full role in rebuilding the safety net of community care. Now is the time to say loud and clear that we believe faith works. Now is the time to tackle the negative media coverage of the church and tell the story once again of faith in action transforming lives and communities.

The Faithworks Movement exists to give you a voice that can be heard in government, to inspire and equip you in your service of your local community and to enable you to join together with tens of thousands of others across the UK to demonstrate that faith works. Alone we will never be heard. But together, by faith, nothing is impossible. Please join us by becoming a member of the Faithworks Movement and declaring to our nation with one voice that faith works!

For more details of how to become a group (a church or project) or individual member of the Faithworks Movement see 6.2: Becoming a Faithworks Member.

1.3: The Faithworks Charter

Adopting a new professionalism is a challenge for us all. We need to work hard to overcome the suspicion that Christian welfare provision is simply proselytism via the back door; that local churches are self-serving and detached from the real needs of the communities they are supposed to be serving; that what we do is short term and amateurish. We need to demonstrate we are already in the forefront of 'hands-on' community welfare across the UK and are now keen to build our capacity and deliver excellent and sustainable life-changing models of care.

That's what the Faithworks Charter is all about. If we are going to work in our communities and in partnership with other agencies and local and national government, we need to be committed to doing so in a professional manner.

As part of the reinvention of public services, politicians are talking about 'public/private partnerships' (PPPs), but the failure of many big corporates to deliver on their promises has not only proved embarrassing, both for them and the government, but has also significantly eroded the public's confidence in these shareholder-driven partnerships.

That is why the Faithworks Movement challenges government to begin talking about 'public/private/non-profit-making partnerships' (PPNPPs) and churches to demonstrate that we can deliver the professional social action, social justice and community building projects that we all need; to demonstrate that we are worth partnering because our motivation and engine is not profit but our faith.

Put together by a team of professionals, including practitioners, church leaders, lawyers and policy-makers, the Faithworks Charter is a 'bench-mark' for local churches, Christian agencies and projects to sign up to and then work hard towards. And as thousands of churches of all denominations, along with Christian community projects and agencies, stand together to deliver this standard of excellence, Christ's church will begin to be taken just as seriously as a key welfare provider of the twenty-first century as we were in centuries past.

THE FAITHWORKS CHARTER

PRINCIPLES FOR CHURCHES AND LOCAL CHRISTIAN AGENCIES COMMITTED TO EXCELLENCE IN COMMUNITY WORK AND SERVICE PROVISION IN THE UK

Motivated by our Christian faith we commit ourselves to serving others by assuring the following standards in all our community work within twelve months of signing this Charter.

Service to the community

1. To serve and to respect all people regardless of their gender, marital status, race, ethnic origin, religion, age, sexual orientation or physical and mental capability.
2. To acknowledge the freedom of people of all faiths or none both to hold and to express their beliefs and convictions respectfully and freely, within the limits of the UK law.
3. Never to impose our Christian faith or belief on others.
4. To develop partnerships with other churches, voluntary groups, statutory agencies and local government wherever appropriate in order to create an effective, integrated service for our clients avoiding unnecessary duplication of resources.
5. To provide and to publicise regular consultation and reporting forums to client groups and the wider community regarding the effective development and delivery of our work and our responsiveness to their actual needs.

Clients, staff and volunteers

1. To create an environment where clients, volunteers and employees are encouraged and enabled to realise their potential.
2. To assist our clients, volunteers and employees to take responsibility for their own learning and development, both through formal and informal training opportunities and ongoing assessment.
3. To develop an organisational culture in which individuals learn from any mistakes made and where excellence and innovation are encouraged and rewarded.
4. To promote the value of a balanced, holistic lifestyle as part

of each individual's overall personal development.

5. To abide by the requirements of employment law in the UK and to implement best employment practices and procedures designed to maintain our distinctive ethos and values.

Management and outcomes

1. To implement a management structure which fosters and encourages participation by staff at all levels in order to facilitate the fulfilment of the project's goals and visions.

2. To set and to review measurable and timed outcomes annually, and regularly to evaluate and monitor our management structure and output, recognising the need for ongoing organisational flexibility, development and good stewardship of resources.

3. To do all we can to ensure that we are not over-dependent on any one source of funding.

4. To implement best practice procedures in terms of Health and Safety and Child Protection in order to protect our staff, volunteers and clients.

5. To handle our funding in a transparent and accountable way and to give relevant people from outside our organisation/project reasonable access to our accounts.

Signed on behalf of:

Organisation/Project ....

Denomination (if appropriate) ....

Address ....

....

.... Postcode ....

Minister/Priest/Leader/Project Manager ....

Address ....

....

Email ....

Tel no ....

Signature ....

Date ....

Please photocopy, complete and return to Nathan Oley, at Faithworks, The Oasis Centre, 115 Southwark Bridge Road, London SE1 0AX.

Let's deliver together

The Faithworks Movement will gather together all signed copies of the charter and personally deliver them to the door of 10 Downing Street as a public declaration that churches, committed to Christian faith-based welfare provision, are serious and professional agencies who are ready, willing and able to impact communities in need.

But before your church or project rushes into signing the charter, take some time to read through the rest of this manual. Not only does it unpack and explain the relevance of each of the charter's clauses, but it also contains all the information you will need to set up and sustain the relevant, best-practice, local social welfare initiatives it speaks of.

It's time for action. Let's seize the moment together.

1.4: Faithworks Unpacked

The aim of this manual is simple: to enable you to respond to the needs of your community in a professional and confident way that demonstrates God's love in a holistic, real and tangible manner, and which results in the establishment of sustainable projects, thus bringing about ongoing, positive change.

Faithworks Unpacked will help you to:

- identify your community's real needs;
- assess with accuracy your church's ability to respond;
- identify practical tools to engage with your community;
- develop your church's potential and capacity to meet community needs;
- build strong partnerships with your local authority and other community groups;
- deliver professional and sustainable community projects.

Just one more thing: a stitch in time saves nine, so resist the inevitable temptation to race ahead without reading the whole of this manual through. It is packed with tips and hints for your journey from initial ideas to a sustainable reality. Most projects that fail do so because of lack of thought and planning at the outset. Quick-fix solutions are easy to set up, but more often than not are ultimately unsuccessful. As Jesus himself once said, building on sand might be quick, easy and cheap, but the wise always build their houses on rock.

Get wise! Get building!

SECTION 2:

Getting Your Church Involved

2.1: Communicating the Vision

So you have a clear vision for the greater community involvement of your church. But just how do you go about turning it into reality? That's what this manual is all about. First, however, if you want your idea to become a genuine church community project, you had better get them involved and owning it right from the start.

Turning your vision into a church vision

Just like snow flakes, no two churches are the same. Every one is unique! This means that the way you communicate your vision for community engagement to your church must be tailored to suit it, rather than some kind of 'off the shelf' solution. How you go about this task will depend on:

● your church's denominational structure and processes;

● your church's size and make up;

● your church's local leadership style and set-up;

● the strength of your relationships and track record.

However, there are a number of general guidelines that, whatever the structures and conventions you need to work within, are guaranteed to help rather than hinder your progress.

1. Talk to your church leader early

Obviously the best time to speak to your leader is at the 'good idea' stage, before your plans are too far developed. If you want your church leader to own this initiative, involve them from the word go. Whatever you do, don't wait until you have your whole strategy mapped out and then expect them, or your church, automatically to buy into what you are doing and back you. In short, however far you've got, get talking now!

● *Book a meeting*. Don't make the mistake of trying to unload your entire vision on the church steps after the Sunday morning service. Give yourself the best chance of getting your ideas across and give your leader the best chance of taking them on board.

● *Plan what you want to communicate*. Remember that leaders are busy, so think about what you want to get across ahead of time and be succinct.

● *Explain your vision*. Clearly explain what you want to do, how you want to do it, who is involved and how far you have got.

● *Ask their advice*. What do they think of your ideas? What do they think is the best way forward? What are the pitfalls to avoid? What issues do they think you need to take on board that you may not have thought about? How does your vision relate to other church plans and overall strategy?

- *Demonstrate your commitment.* Just about every other person has some great idea for changing the world that they want someone else to be responsible for. Most church leaders already have a very full agenda. So make it clear that you are not trying to dump work on them, but that you are committed to working hard on this yourself.

- *Make yourself accountable.* Listen to their advice. Make it clear that you are not asking for a blank cheque and that you want to work within the church structures.

- *Ask about the next step.* Where should you take the idea from here? Ask if you can present the idea to the church leadership team or decision-making body.

2. Present your vision to the church decision-making body

Make sure you are:

- *Informative.* Explain your vision, your aims and the need. Stand up, speak up and then shut up!

- *Realistic.* Be prepared to answer questions and don't be upset if some of these sound negative. People need time to process information and ideas.

- *Flexible.* Listen to and be prepared to take on board the comments and insights of others. Iron sharpens iron, so listen particularly hard to the people who ask the toughest questions. What are their worries? Have you really thought about them?

- *Accountable.* Seek their formal consent to move from the 'good idea' stage into the initial work phase. Ask them if they will agree in principle to progress your idea in the knowledge that more specific details will be brought back to them for closer scrutiny at a later date.

- *Proactive.* Suggest that a working group (see 3.2: Where to Begin) carries out a community audit/research project (see Section 3: Researching Your Community).

- *Involving.* How would they like to be represented on the project working group? What is their view on its make-up? It is important, if possible, that they have at least one member on it to act as a link person.

3. Communicate with the whole church regularly

Once the research has been completed and the church's governing group has agreed its findings, it is important to present it and the vision to the whole church at an appropriate point. This might be at:

- a Sunday service;
- a special meeting;
- a regular church meeting of some sort.

With the agreement of the church leaders it might be appropriate to circulate your research and proposal, or better still a two-page summary of it, as widely as possible ahead of any meeting that takes place (or alternatively directly after an initial presentation has been made). This gives people an opportunity to think over and reflect on it.

Remember that giving notice of a meeting well ahead of

time will also help to make people feel involved, even if they are not able to make it. The one thing that you want to avoid after all your hard work is people feeling excluded or rushed into making a decision.

Make sure that you do the following:

- Carry forward all the lessons from your earlier presentations to your church leader and its decision-making team (see above).

- Confirm your church leader(s) is happy with what you are planning to present to the church, before you present it. Think about the implications of what you are planning to say. For instance, it would be inappropriate to appeal for money without first clearing this.

- Let people know how they can get involved. Are you looking for volunteers, working group members, prayer support, finance, etc?

- Keep the whole church informed, involved and inspired on a regular basis. It is hard work, but it will pay huge dividends along the way.

SECTION 3:

Researching Your Community

3.1: Why Research?

If it isn't broken, don't fix it! Or, put another way, before your church goes steaming into setting up an elaborate scheme to house the homeless, develop an after-school club or establish a family centre, it pays to stop long enough to ask if any of that is what the local community actually needs!

It should go without saying that the people who know a community best are the people who are part of it. However, planners and politicians are only recently beginning to wake up to the fact that the active participation of local people in determining the future of their own communities is crucial. By virtue of who they are, local people have a depth of insight about, not to mention a vested interest in, the development of their community.

A local church may already consider itself to have a fair 'intuitive' understanding of its surrounding community, but it's never wise to be presumptuous. Nothing beats the foundation of good community research. It will either serve to objectively confirm your present views and instincts or throw up some big surprises to correct them.

Either way, you've made some real progress.

Investment in quality community research is never a wasted exercise if you are serious about making a difference. It will:

- deepen your understanding of your community;
- ensure potential projects meet real needs;
- maintain your focus on people before projects;
- create a sense of local ownership and participation;
- provide necessary information for potential sponsors;
- avoid unnecessary duplication of provision;
- give local people a say in the future of their community.

3.2: Where to Begin

Forming a working group

Good research of the needs of your community will take time, energy and commitment, as well as some financial investment. Your success will be dependent on putting together a working group with the right mix of skills, which will include those of networking and presentation, as well as administration and the technical aspects of research evaluation.

This group may be entirely 'in house', but you may choose to involve representatives from other churches and/or local voluntary organisations, which not only enables the effective sharing of resources but has the added benefit of beginning to build healthy partnerships and strong relationships in the community for the future. Talk this through with your church leader/leadership team for their approval.

Terms of reference for the working group

'Terms of reference' sounds very formal but these simply ensure consistency in understanding. Get them approved by your church's decision-making body. They could include:

- the purpose and scope of the community research project;
- which constituent parts of the church or other organisations the members should be drawn from;
- length of time of the study;
- reporting process – when and how.

How to begin

Having established your working group, your first task is to define the community that your research will cover. The most obvious way to do this is to select a specific geographical area, such as the parish your church is in, a particular housing estate, etc. But it's also important to understand that different types of community boundaries exist that may not be obvious or 'official'. Sometimes recognised political boundaries between wards, local authorities or parishes have little significance for residents. To help your research you need to ascertain where the community perceives boundaries to exist. These may include railway lines, rivers, busy main roads or housing estates. Sometimes these coincide with political boundaries, but more often not. Getting these boundaries wrong will blur and distort your findings.

Once you have established the geographical community you want to audit, your task is then to ask yourselves whether the research you are interested in requires a general overview or a focus on a particular group defined by age, socio-economic differences, ethnic origin, gender, etc.

Alternatively, you might want to explore a key theme such as health, unemployment or education. But remember: for the research to be manageable, the size of the area/sample chosen should reflect the available time and resources of your team.

3.3: Gathering Information

The information you need to collect falls into two categories:

- *'Hard' data.* Facts and statistics about the community generally, such as population, housing, businesses, community organisations, recreational facilities and local services, or specifically relating to the particular issue you are hoping to tackle.
- *'Soft' data.* Local views, opinions, attitudes, perspectives and feelings about the area and specifically the issues you want to research.

The best studies will contain a mixture of both 'hard' and 'soft' information, each informing the other. What people say when giving their opinion may well be very different from statistical information about how they live out their lives. But before embarking on a time-consuming round of surveying and consulting, it is well worth finding out what information already exists. You don't want to waste your time simply duplicating it.

'Hard' data sources

Good places from which to gather 'hard' data include:

- *The census.* Available in your local library, this will give you detailed demographic information, e.g. age groups, ethnic mix, employment details. The drawback is that it is only published every ten years, but the latest census information will be available late 2002/2003.

- *Indices of deprivation.* Measures of deprivation for every ward and local authority area in England are available online from the Department of Transport, Local Government and Regions (DTLR): www.regeneration. dtlr.gov.uk/research. (Also see 5.10: Working with National Government.)

- *Local authority and statutory agencies.* A great deal of information on your community will be available from the various local statutory bodies, e.g. Social Services and the Health Authority. Contact your local council and ask what studies have been carried out and how you can access the information. (See also 5.11: Working with Local Government.)

- *The police.* Contact them for crime statistics, vandalism, crime prevention initiatives, community problems, etc.

- *The Early Years Development and Childcare Partnership* (Local Childcare Partnerships in Scotland). They have statistics relating to children in the area.

- *Local Council for Voluntary Service (CVS).* Ask what relevant reports they know about or have access to, as well as if other community groups have carried out recent surveys of your area.

- *The Internet.* This is also a useful source of information. Look at sites such as www.upmystreet.com, or type your town name on a search engine. You'll be surprised what you can find out about your locality.

- Other specialist groups you might find helpful include housing associations, adult education and voluntary organisations.

'Soft' data sources

Having gathered your 'hard' data, now ask yourself what 'soft' data you need to complete a balanced picture of your community. Facts and figures go some way towards describing local life, but to grasp a more detailed and accurate picture you will need to talk to the community and include their stories, opinions, viewpoints and outlooks.

3.4: 'Soft' Research Tools

It is vital to give your 'soft' research 'breadth' and 'depth'. There is a wide range of quantity (or breadth) and quality (or depth) techniques and tools for community research. For instance, while questionnaires will give you breadth of information, depth will come from interviewing a smaller carefully selected sample, running focus groups, etc. Combining the breadth of questionnaires with the depth of information that can be gained from interviews and focus groups will always give you a clearer indication of the real needs of your community and so facilitate a more efficient response to them.

The following pages contain information about how to put together and use a selection of the best tried and tested 'soft' research tools.

(a) QUESTIONNAIRES

Questionnaires are the quickest way of gathering basic, broad brush stroke, 'quantity' type information about your community, and are very useful for that reason.

But bear in mind the following:

1. Careful planning is needed to ensure that information collected is clear, meaningful and suitable for analysis. Multiple choice questions where interviewees answer by selecting A, B, C or D, for example, are by far the easiest to collate.

2. Your questionnaire needs to be simple and short, to flow naturally and to include monitoring information (e.g. age, sex, etc.). Any controversial or difficult questions should be left until the end.

3. It's essential to run a 'test' on a small but representative group of people first to ensure that your questions are clear and that the answers can be accurately analysed and provide useful feedback.

4. Make sure that the people you survey know who you are, why you are asking them for information, what you will be doing with it and how and when they can access the results.

5. Hold a training session for all those who will use your questionnaire. Give them a chance to practise using it on one another and carefully explain how to deal with the different reactions they are likely to get to it.

6. Questionnaires are far more successful when someone proactively carries out the interviews rather than leaving forms and then expecting people to complete and return them.

7. Think about places where you might conduct interviews, e.g. door to door, the local shopping centre, train station, youth club, toddler group, etc.

8. If your questionnaire is designed for the whole community rather than a specific group, you should ensure that the sample size questioned is representative of the local population.

Reasons for using questionnaires

These include:

- Information can be given anonymously.
- You get precise answers to defined questions.
- You can contact large numbers of people.
- You can make comparisons between different groups of people within the survey.

However, questionnaires do have their shortcomings and so should always be used in conjunction with other 'quality' tools to provide depth and accuracy. If used on their own they can even be quite misleading for the following reasons:

- Most people are naturally suspicious of strangers asking them questions, so the answers can be inspired by all sorts of motives, e.g. 'How do I get rid of this person as soon as possible?', 'I'm not telling him what I really think – it will be used against me', 'I don't like these people prying into my life', 'What is all this information going to be used for?', etc.
- People are often busy when you call on them or stop them in the street and preoccupied with other issues.
- There are two types of questionnaire (see Figures 1 and

2). The first (Figure 1) allows for ease of analysis but may make people feel boxed in if the selection of possible answers your questionnaire presents doesn't fully cater for their views. People's answers may be option 'E' when you've only offered them A, B, C or D!

- If you use a questionnaire that doesn't have tick boxes (Figure 2), not only does this make it much harder to analyse but, because you can still only allow for one- or two-line answers, you still lack depth of feedback.

- If not designed with appropriate sensitivity, a questionnaire can be intrusive and therefore result in interviewees choosing to be evasive or dishonest.

Designing a questionnaire – the basic rules

- Make sure the instructions are clear.
- Keep the layout simple.
- Use simple language.
- Keep it short, ideally one sheet of paper.
- Make it flow naturally.
- Put controversial/difficult questions at the end.
- Be consistent in the terms you use.
- Avoid ambiguous terms that may mean different things to different people.
- Don't ask leading questions, e.g. 'How has the one-way system complicated life?' Instead ask, 'What impact has the introduction of the one-way system had?'
- Include monitoring information (i.e. age, sex, etc.) at the end.

● See the two sample questionnaires below (Figures 1 and 2).

Figure 1

Buryborough Community Questionnaire

1. How long have you lived in Buryborough?
   - ☐ Under 1 year
   - ☐ Under 5 years
   - ☐ Under 10 years
   - ☐ Over 10 years

2. How would you rate Buryborough's youth facilities?
   - ☐ Excellent
   - ☐ Good
   - ☐ Adequate
   - ☐ Poor

3. Do you think that this situation is:
   - ☐ Improving?
   - ☐ Unchanging?
   - ☐ Deteriorating?

4. Which age group do you think is best catered for?
   - ☐ Under 10s
   - ☐ 10–14s
   - ☐ 15–17s
   - ☐ 18–23s

5. Which age group do you think has the worst provision?
   - ☐ Under 10s
   - ☐ 10–14s

☐   15–17s
☐   18–23s

6. What new facilities would you most like to see for young people in Buryborough?

7. What is your age group?
    ☐   Under 14
    ☐   15–17
    ☐   18–23
    ☐   Over 23

8. Sex?
    ☐   Male   ☐   Female

Figure 2

Buryborough Community Questionnaire

1. What do you most enjoy about life in Buryborough?

2. What would you most like to change about life in Buryborough?

3. What is the biggest issue that Buryborough faces?

4. What is the biggest issue that you think the young people in the community face?

5. What is the biggest issue that you think faces the elderly in the community?

6. Name

7. Address

8. Age group
   ☐ 14–18
   ☐ 19–25
   ☐ 26–40
   ☐ 41–65
   ☐ 66+

9. Sex:
   ☐ Male   ☐ Female

(b) INTERVIEWS

Interviews are much looser than questionnaires and therefore enable a much broader exploration of ideas and opinions. They will also provide you with more quality or depth of insight and information. They are more personal and have the added advantage that you can probe by asking supplementary questions where appropriate. Although they are time consuming, interviews are an excellent way to discover more about the life of the community. Use them to question teachers, social workers, playgroup leaders, youth workers, doctors, other service providers, residents – in fact anyone you believe will have a depth of insight into the specific issue you are researching.

Pros

- More personal approach.
- Allow you to probe and ask supplementary questions where necessary.
- Don't require literacy.
- Interviewees feel they're involved in problem-solving.

Cons

- No anonymity.
- Time consuming, for those being interviewed as well as for the interviewer(s).
- The interviewer may influence the answers.

Designing an interview

- Start with a brief introduction explaining who you are and the purpose of the interview.
- Establish some relevant background information about the interviewee, such as what their role/participation in the community is and how long they have lived/worked in the community.
- Follow this with a series of questions grouped under key themes. Use these as a guide and discussion starter for supplementary questions.

Basic rules for conducting interviews

- Clearly explain the context of the interview.

- Confirm how much time the interviewee has to give. Don't overrun.

- Be respectful.

- Have your questions prepared and ready.

- Use open questions such as Who? Why? What? When? Where? How?

- Keep your questions simple.

- Don't butt in. Leave time for your interviewee to respond.

- Never finish an interviewee's sentence for them as you may miss the heart of what they have to say.

- Don't be afraid of silence – allow your interviewee time to think.

- Be flexible and spontaneous. Ask follow-up questions.

- Actively listen to all that the interviewee has to say.

- Don't be afraid to ask the same question more than once in a different way.

- If you don't quite understand an answer, use devices like 'So what you are saying is. . .' or 'Could you tell me more about that?' to draw out more information.

- Be sure to focus on solutions as well as the problems.

- Make brief notes during the interview. Verbatim transcripts are not useful.

- Don't just note down the issues you agree with, but make sure you note every point made.

- Write up the notes as soon as you can after the interview, while it is still fresh.

(c) PARTICIPATORY APPRAISAL METHODS

Participatory appraisal methods of community research are visual, creative and interactive. Those who take part are free to control their own level and extent of participation, are not compelled to disclose personal information and can even remain anonymous.

'Planning for Real'

'Planning for Real' is a good example of a participatory appraisal method of research. It is eye-catching and very 'hands-on', allowing people to have a real say about what they feel about their neighbourhood.

It involves creating a drawing or, if you are really ambitious, a 3D model of the community onto which you then invite people to stick notes that express their views about the features of the neighbourhood. Once attached, a note becomes anonymous, thus allowing people who may not feel at ease with openly discussing their views a chance to have their say.

Be creative about how to get as many people as possible involved. Consider using a busy public place such as a shopping precinct. Another option is to take your drawing or model on a tour of local groups and services, such as youth clubs, day centres for older people and parent/carer and toddler groups. This way you should get the views of a good representative sample of the whole community.

One group invited parents in their local community to

select and pin cards onto two specially designed consultation boards, the first in the shape of a brick wall for problems and the other in the shape of a fish for wishes. These were set up in public places, such as the leisure centre and shopping precinct. Some of the cards were pre-written with specific commonly felt problems, others with possible improvements that could be made. There were also blank cards that people could write on. Once someone had selected a card and pinned it to the appropriate board others who agreed with their comment could 'vote' for it by sticking another pin into the card. At the end of the exercise all the pins were counted and the most popular ideas for improvements and the most often experienced problems were easily identified.

'Planning for Real' was devised by the Neighbourhood Initiatives Foundation. Contact them for more information about its use. (For address see Resources and contacts, p.68.)

(d) FOCUS GROUPS

Through informal chats, interviews, the use of your questionnaire and so on you will have come across a number of people with lots of good things to say about the area of research you are involved with. A focus group gives you the chance to get more out of them in the context of a group discussion.

Invite possible candidates to a meal (e.g. buffet or barbecue), including the opportunity to discuss in depth the topic that concerns you. Use the information you have built up from your questionnaire to prime discussion. Alternatively, contact specific local community groups who you think will have something to say on the issues you are looking at, and ask whether they will give you a couple of hours to talk with them.

A focus group provides the following:

- A creative opportunity for high quality interaction.

- The synergy of bouncing individual ideas and opinions off a group to produce a deeper understanding.

- Quick access to a large volume of information and depth of insight.

- Immediate checks and balances on participants' comments, views and opinions.

- An easier environment for those who may feel threatened in a 'one to one' situation to be more open.

A facilitator's guide to focus groups

- Apply all the interview principles set out on page 59.

- The ideal size of a focus group is between six and ten people. It should never be more than twelve.

- Don't allow one or two people to dominate.

- Give everyone the opportunity to contribute.

- Use the question 'What do others think?' often.

- Don't be confrontational.

- Check your understanding by regularly pausing, reviewing and clarifying the discussion up to that point.

- Prevent the discussion going round in circles by summing up and explaining that it is time to move on.

- Use someone else to take detailed notes. This allows you to concentrate on directing the conversation and involving all the participants, without having to worry about getting all that is said down on paper.

3.5: A Five-step Research Plan

Here's one idea of how to combine quantity and quality in a five-step research plan.

1. 'Quantity' research

- Use a questionnaire (see 3.4(a)) to ask your chosen sample number of respondents what they think about the needs of the community. What are the major issues? Remember, you are not looking for depth but rather overview and feelings.

2. Review

Analyse your findings and focus on the core issues you want to tackle. Do this by:

- collating and listing the different needs and issues that your research has identified;
- ranking them in order of importance to those your research brought you into contact with;

- identifying the three or four core areas in which you want to do more research.

3. 'Quality' research

- Identify the groups and individuals most affected by the issues your initial research revealed. Spend more time talking with them by using an appropriate (quality) research tool. What is their view? What insights do they have? What would they like to see happen? Why?

- Talk to the people who are at the heart of the community, the 'gatekeepers': the GP, teacher, school governor, business leader, job centre manager, social worker, police sergeant, community police officer, shopkeeper, publican, milkman, etc. Listen hard to what they say. They live and breathe local life.

4. Review

In the light of what you have now heard, identify the way ahead.

5. Consult

Are your conclusions correct? Go back to some of those you talked with, as well as those with experience from outside the community, to test your ideas. Be prepared to amend your conclusions in the light of these discussions.

3.6: Analysing Your Data

By now you will have built up a lot of data about the life of your community in general or the specific issue you have been researching. However, in order to complete your analysis so that it provides you with meaningful information that will act as a springboard to future action, as a group ask yourselves the following kinds of questions:

- What is life like here?
- What is life like for specific people?
- Who benefits most from this area?
- Who benefits least from this area?
- What are people's needs?
- What are their opportunities?
- Where are the gaps in provision?
- Who wins?
- Who loses?
- Who decides?
- What ideas for solutions have been put forward so far?

A community report

Now write up your conclusions as a report in a clear, accessible and imaginative style. Use visuals, maps and diagrams so that the information you have gained will be accessible and easily understood. A suggested layout of your report is as follows:

- Title.
- Acknowledgements – thank everyone who contributed and stress the value of the process; of listening and working together being an important part of what you did.
- List of contents.
- Introduction – explain why you have compiled the report; what it aims to do.
- Methods – describe the various research methods you used.
- Main findings – use headings for the different areas.
- Main issues – give a summary and analysis of your findings.
- Future development – suggest recommendations for action, resources needed, possible sources of resources; key players; timeframe for development, etc.
- Brief summary/conclusion.
- How to give feedback on the report, get involved, etc.
- Appendices – give a list of sources, people involved, copies of questionnaires, maps, etc.

Where now?

Don't let your work gather dust and stagnate. Present it to your church leadership team/decision-making body. Think about who else would benefit from reading it. Remember that it is not an end in itself but a vital tool in the regenerative process of your community. As such it should form the basis of an ongoing dialogue about, and with, your community and could also serve as a valuable contribution to your Local Strategic Partnership (see 5.11: Working with Local Government).

RESOURCES AND CONTACTS

The Neighbourhood Initiatives Foundation
The Poplars
Lightmoor
Telford TF4 3QN
Tel: 0870 7700339
Website: www.nif.co.uk
National organisation supporting the active participation of communities in their development, including 'Planning for Real' consultation exercises, publications and training.

New Economics Foundation (NEF)
Cinnamon House
6–8 Cole Street
London SE1 4YH
Tel: 020 7407 7447
Website: www.neweconomics.org.uk
Independent think tank. Training, research, publications, etc. Contact for information on community participation.

National Association of Councils for Voluntary Service
(NACVS)
3rd Floor
Arundel Court
177 Arundel Street
Sheffield S1 2NU
Tel: 0114 278 6636
Website: www.nacvs.org.uk
Umbrella organisation for Councils for Voluntary Service
(CVS). Contact to find your local CVS.

Southwark Diocesan Board for Church in Society
Trinity House
4 Chapel Court
Borough High Street
London SE1 1HW
Tel: 020 7403 8686
Publications, including *The Parish Profile Pack*. Census
information by parish, etc.

Further reading

Community Profiling: Auditing Social Needs by Murray
Hawtin, Geraint Hughes and Janie Percy-Smith (Open
University Press, 1994).

Getting to Know Your Neighbours – Engaging with your community and researching community needs, a practical guide for Christian groups (Shaftesbury Society, 1999).

The Parish Profile Pack (Southwark Diocesan Board for
Church in Society, 1995).

Participation Works! – 21 techniques of community participation for the 21st century (New Economics Foundation, 1998).

SECTION 4:

Developing Your Strategy

4.1: Why Plan?

You've carried out an audit of your community, researched its needs and identified the issues you feel passionate about. Now it's time to begin planning your response.

Three planning myths

Planning is unspiritual

For some, the whole idea of strategic planning feels just a little 'unspiritual'. Are we selling out to secular management gurus and techniques that deny God's Spirit the room to lead us? What's wrong with having the objective to 'let go and let God'?

Ironically, to see life in these terms, far from being biblical, is to fall for the old dualism that has dogged the church for centuries – the division of the sacred from the secular, faith from fact, science from religion.

God himself is a strategist and a planner. You only have to read Paul's opening statements to the Ephesians to be aware of that fact. And what of Paul himself? His aim was to preach the gospel in Rome (see Romans 1:13), and to get there he laid out some very specific objectives.

Far from destroying our faith, setting realistic but challenging goals and objectives helps it to flourish. As you reach them, all those involved with your project will be encouraged and enthused to believe, to pray and to work for more success. At the end of the day goals and objectives are simply statements of faith (see Philippians 3:13–14). We believe that this is what God wants us to do and we trust him to achieve his purposes through us.

Planning is too difficult

Some people are afraid of the planning process because it seems too complicated and difficult. Even the phrase 'strategic planning' strikes fear into their hearts, let alone mention of 'measurable objectives' and 'budgets'. But, in truth, projects that are poorly planned are far more demanding, difficult and ultimately disillusioning to run. Planning is the most effective route to getting the job done as quickly, efficiently and simply as possible. However difficult planning a project might appear to be, trying to tackle it without doing so is infinitely harder and very frustrating.

Planning wastes time

Some people view the very idea of sitting through a planning process as a giant delaying tactic on the part of those who lack vision. Planning is another term for procrastination. 'Let's stop talking and just get on with it!' they say. However, the truth is that time spent in planning is never wasted and in fact will eventually deliver the project far more effectively and sustainably than an 'eyes-wide-shut' approach.

The planning process:

- Clarifies goals.
- Develops the vision.
- Maximises both human and financial resources.
- Ensures direction.
- Allocates responsibilities.
- Identifies risks.
- Achieves the best results.
- Facilitates building a team.
- Develops ownership.
- Communicates the vision to others.
- Raises expectations.

4.2: The Project Team

As a first step in your planning process put together a project group of between four and eight people, with a skill set appropriate to the task you are considering. You will need a mix of skills but it is vital, of course, that each group member shares the same basic vision.

Working in a strong and carefully chosen team will compensate for weaknesses and optimise strengths and therefore give your project the best opportunity for success. Once you have built your team you can begin the journey that will turn your dream into reality with confidence.

It sounds obvious, but the project team should be made up of those with the necessary skills and time to steer your strategy forward and bring the vision to life. Don't fall into the trap of appointing people because of their status. Instead choose members for what they can contribute.

Just as with the formation of the working group for your community research project, ensure that your church leadership team/governing body is happy with your proposed group make-up. Agree some written terms of reference for the group with a report back deadline.

Suggested members of the steering group might include the following:

- The team leader.
- At least one member of the church's decision-making body to act as a link person between the two groups.
- Someone with experience/professional skill in the main function of the proposed project, e.g. a youth worker for a youth project.
- A person with finance/accounting skills.
- A person with PR skills.
- A future member/user of the project.
- Church administrator/member of admin team.
- A manager/planner.
- Some of the people from the working group for your community research who are keen to stay involved.

4.3: The Strategy Wheel

The Strategy Wheel is a simple strategic planning tool. Used carefully it will help you to successfully navigate your journey from your starting point to your destination.

The Strategy Wheel is also an effective planning tool. Just like any wheel, it is perpetual. The process of planning is never completed – it is an ongoing task.

Figure 3

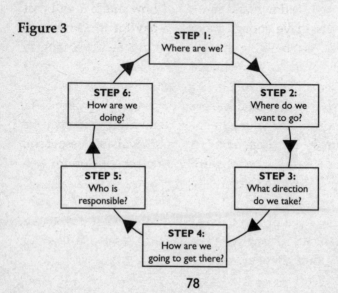

(a) STEP 1: WHERE ARE WE?

Diagnosing your situation

An accurate assessment of your starting point and available resources is essential before beginning any journey. This takes discipline and some restraint, especially for those entrepreneurial types who find it hard to wait for tomorrow. However, without giving time to this first step, ultimately you are very likely to end up frustrated and disillusioned, leaving the needs of your community unmet.

As the country yokel said to the city gent, 'If you want to get to the manor, you don't want to start from here.' But of course 'here' is the only point you can start from! The most detailed map in the world won't get you to where you want to go if you can't first pinpoint where it is you are starting from – that basic but essential piece of information.

Jesus told his disciples a story: 'Suppose one of you wants to build a tower. What is the first thing you will do? Won't you sit down and figure out how much it will cost and if you have enough money to pay for it? Otherwise, you will start building the tower, but not be able to finish. Then everyone who sees what is happening will laugh at you' (see Luke 14:28–29). You may have the vision to establish a 24-hour-a-day, seven-days-a-week drop-in and advice centre for young people in an empty pub on your high street. But depending on your available resources, perhaps running a twice weekly, after-school club for two hours is a good first step.

ACTION: As a project team, invest some quality time in a thorough SWOT analysis. Set aside at least one hour to thinking through your:

Strengths
Weaknesses
Opportunities
Threats

Assess where your church is right now. What skills and resources are at your disposal within your group, the church and the wider community? List them on a flip chart or white board to build up a clear and accurate picture of where you are and what kind of response you are capable of.

(b) STEP 2: WHERE DO WE WANT TO GO?

Identifying your vision and aims

Where are you headed? What's your destination? As management guru, Steve Covey, puts it, 'Begin [your journey] with the end in mind.'

Your community research (see Section 3: Researching Your Community) will have provided you with a clear idea of your local needs, as well as the gaps in provision and facilities. As you match these needs against your vision and resources, your aim(s) will gradually become focused.

Many community projects fail because they lack clarity and definition about exactly what it is they are trying to achieve. If you set out on a journey not knowing your precise destination, you'll probably never arrive there! Where are you aiming to get to? Now is the moment to define your overall vision or mission and your central aims.

A vision/mission statement

Your vision/mission is the overall purpose or reason for your project. Of course, in one sense you already know exactly what that is – it is what has brought you this far. But now it is good to clarify it by writing it down in an agreed way in the form of a vision or mission statement.

> **Faithworks Mission Statement**
>
> To put Christian faith back into the heart of the public sphere.

Your aims

Aims are short and broad statements or sentences that sum up the direction of your project and set out the main ways or boundaries within which you will operate to achieve your vision/mission. They are long term. They should define the key areas in which you want to work; the basic issues that you are committed to addressing.

> The aims of Faithworks are:
> 1. To empower and inspire every local church to rediscover its role as the hub of the community.
> 2. To challenge and change the public perception of the church by engaging with both media and government.
> 3. To promote Christian values within our society.

ACTION: As a project team, come up with a vision/

mission statement and a set of aims with which you are happy. The best way to do this is to work with a white board or flip chart. Give enough time for everyone to make a good contribution to the discussion. Having agreed your statement and aims, give yourselves a bit of time to think them through again before finally committing yourselves to them at a second meeting.

(c) STEP 3: WHAT DIRECTION DO WE TAKE?

Setting your objectives

Having established where you are and where you want to go, now is the time to plan your route. One of the keys to success for any community project is to accurately map the detail of your pathway. Break your aim(s) down into a progression of smaller, measurable and achievable objectives. Objectives are the steps along your route that you follow in order to reach your destination. However far ahead you've set your sights, the only way to get there is one step at a time.

Your objectives are the specific short-term targets (up to two years ahead as an absolute maximum) that you set for yourself on the way to achieving your aim(s). Each objective should be SMART: specific, measurable, attainable, relevant and time-specific:

Specific   Your objectives must be focused and clear.
Measurable   Your objectives must be quantifiable. You should always know whether or not they have been achieved without any kind of ambiguity.

Attainable　　　Your objectives must be realistic – challenging but possible rather than idealistic but impossible.

Relevant　　　Your objectives must be relevant to your overall aim rather than a pleasant distraction or red herring.

Time-specific　　Your objectives must have realistic deadlines that you aim to stick to. 'As soon as possible' breeds the kind of fuzziness that makes any progress, or lack of it, difficult, if not impossible, to evaluate.

ACTION: Using the flip chart or white board once more, get your project team to write a series of specific objectives for each of your aims. Check that each one is SMART.

(d) STEP 4: HOW ARE WE GOING TO GET THERE?

Fixing your task and activities

The clearer you are about how you are going to achieve your aims, the easier you will find them to achieve. So, having established your objectives, now is the time to break each of them down even further into a set of smaller, bite-sized tasks and activities. These are the individual actions that your team needs to accomplish in order for your SMART objectives to be realised.

The clearer you are concerning this process, the more effective you will be in achieving your objectives. Your task is to drive out any fuzziness or muddledness that might still exist about the way ahead.

ACTION: As a project team, brainstorm all that needs to be done in order to achieve each of your objectives, and then agree the key tasks that must be completed for it to happen. Lastly, don't forget to timetable each of these individual tasks so you can assess your progress.

(e) STEP 5: WHO IS RESPONSIBLE?

Implementing your decisions

Having put Steps 1–4 of your strategic plan in place, now it is time to nail things down. Who needs to do what in order for your objectives and activities to be achieved? Where does the buck stop on each individual task? Without completing this essential step of holding specific individuals responsible and accountable for particular tasks, even the greatest plan in the world runs the risk of never being realised.

ACTION: Allocate the individual tasks to team members. You can choose to ask someone beyond the group to do a task, but a member of the project team must still remain responsible for ensuring its accomplishment on time.

Now use all the information you have to plan your 'Critical Path Analysis' (CPA), or schedule (see 4.4: Keeping Records).

(f) STEP 6: HOW ARE WE DOING?

Monitoring your progress

Monitoring is the process of regularly checking and reflecting on your progress against your strategy. It is vital to constantly monitor how you are doing against the objectives you have been pursuing. Effective monitoring answers essential questions about how things are developing, which allows you to identify your strengths and weaknesses, successes and failings, opportunities and problems sooner rather than later. This in turn means that you can positively respond to them by adjusting your objectives and strategy as necessary.

Though the planning process is invaluable it must always be your servant, never your master. Don't ever let it become a strait-jacket in which you trap yourself. The planning process is essential, but your plans should always be flexible. Changing circumstances will inevitably necessitate adjustments to your approach in order that you successfully make it to your destination.

ACTION: Your project team should meet regularly to monitor and assess your progress. When you do, ask yourselves whether:

- the activities you have set are being carried out on time;
- you are still on track to achieve your objectives;
- there are any problems you need to tackle;
- you need any shift of emphasis;
- you are overstretching yourselves;
- you need more resources.

There will always be setbacks and disappointments on any journey, so when targets are not achieved within the agreed timetable, view it as part of a learning curve and ask yourselves the following questions:

- Why did we fail to hit our target?
- What problems did we ignore or underestimate?
- Were the reasons for failure inside or outside our team's control?
- Could the problems have been foreseen?
- How can the problems be overcome?

Setting a strategic plan is never a one-off task. The accomplishment of any goal is really about ongoing reassessment and adjustment as a result of forever changing conditions and circumstances. So review and revise your plan in the light of what you have learned by moving on from Step 6 back round to Step 1 of the Strategy Wheel and then back on through each successive step in exactly the same way as before.

4.4: Keeping Records

So you have agreed your overall vision and aims; you have developed your SMART objectives, worked out the individual tasks and activities required to fulfil them and gone on to allocate who is responsible for their delivery (see 4.3: The Strategy Wheel). Now you have to make sure you don't fall at the final hurdle by keeping an accurate, agreed and regularly reviewed record or schedule of action.

Getting started

- Some people prefer diagrams and flow charts, others are more list orientated and others like tables. Just pick a system that suits you. There is no wrong or right way of doing this. All that is important is that you find an effective way, which suits your team, to keep a track of where you are going, when you need to action things and who is taking responsibility for doing so.

- One person (your team leader or manager) should take responsibility for record-taking, so there is one definitive up-to-date, centrally held set. Copies should be made for each team member.

- Remember: records merely reflect your vision, aims and objectives, and because they are all amendable and flexible, your records should be as well.

The following is a simple and manageable way of keeping an effective record of schedule without getting bogged down in jargon and technical complexity! A simple Excel spreadsheet or Word table will help you do the job.

Recording the overall picture

- Depict your vision, aims and objectives in a diagrammatic form, so you can regularly remind yourself of why you started all this in the first place! (See Figure 4.)
- Use the chart to regularly ask yourself how your tasks/activities fulfil your objectives, your objectives fulfil your aims and your aims fulfil your overall vision.

Figure 4

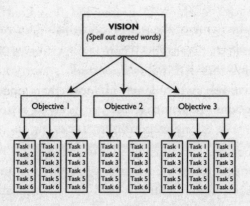

- You may choose to have more than six tasks for each division of each objective, you may have less. This is just to give you an idea.
- You may also choose not to divide each objective into different tiers of task, but it may help to separate categories.

Recording the big picture

It is important to keep an overall record of the big picture. This is called a CPA (Critical Path Analysis). Table 1 is a suggested way of doing this.

- Produce a Word table, with months across the top of the page. A year's worth is helpful for planning ahead.

- Down the left-hand side, put your key objectives in alphabetical order.

- In each box across the page, put your specific tasks/activities in the relevant month.

- Put tasks that are 'set in stone' in bold and capitals to distinguish from those that are movable, for which you should use lower case.

- Add the name of the person responsible for each objective under that objective title, so everyone knows where the buck stops.

- Some tasks may appear in more than one row for clarity.

- Table 1 shows the end point of each objective within the process.

Table 1

CPA

OBJECTIVE	APR 02	MAY 02	JUN 02	JUL 02	AUG 02	SEP 02
Communicating with the church (Dave)				• FINAL SIGN OFF FROM CHURCH FOR OPENING CENTRE		
External partnerships (Hannah)				• AGREEMENT ON PARTNERSHIP		
Funding (Sarah)						• FUNDING FOR YEAR I SECURED
Marketing (Becca)						
Programme (John)						
Training (Peter)						• FINAL STAFF & VOLUNTEER TRAINING
Venue (Sue)						

OBJECTIVE	OCT 02	NOV 02	DEC 02	JAN 03	FEB 03	MAR 03
Communicating with the church (Dave)						
External partnerships (Hannah)						
Funding (Sarah)						
Marketing (Becca)				• LAUNCH PROJECT		
Programme (John)	• FINAL PROGRAMME OF EVENTS AGREED					
Training (Peter)						
Venue (Sue)			• VENUE OPERATIONAL			

- Table 2 on the following page shows the complete CPA, which has the various stages you need to record in order to achieve the end point of each as outlined in Table 1. These stages may not appear in bold and capitals, as they may not be set in stone.

- Review your big picture by checking down the columns for each month. If you have too many activities happening at the same time, or you require more planning time between each objective, this process will highlight your problem ahead of time and allow you to adjust your schedule so that you can sustain the workload with the resources you have available. Amend your timings as necessary.

- Once you have your CPA record complete, don't keep it a secret. The idea is to make sure all the key people who are involved in the project agree with the records and own them.

KEY POINT: A CPA must be a flexible and regularly reviewed document in order for it to be of use to you.

Table 2

CPA

OBJECTIVE	APR 02	MAY 02	JUN 02	JUL 02	AUG 02	SEP 02
Communicating with the church (Dave)	• 1st meeting to discuss plans	• 2nd meeting with leadership team	• 3rd meeting with whole church	• **FINAL SIGN OFF FROM CHURCH FOR OPENING CENTRE**	• Ongoing communication	→
External partnerships (Hannah)	• Meeting to discuss plans	• Follow-up to 1st meeting	• Document to outline partnership	• **AGREEMENT ON PARTNERSHIP**	• Ongoing communication	→
Funding (Sarah)	• Research opportunities – trusts, local businesses, etc.	• Further research • Draft proposal document/ballpark budget and circulate	• Assess response	• Further opportunities explored • Income received	• Further follow-up	• **FUNDING FOR YEAR I SECURED**
Marketing (Becca)			• First marketing plan drafted	• Marketing plan agreed	• Opportunities researched	• Finalise plan/lists • Book key staff/contributors for launch
Programme (John)	• Research programme to meet needs	• More research	• Test ideas with groups of young people	• Cost each programme and produce timetable • Research equipment needs	• Plan equipment location in venue • Draft of ideas to team • Approval of programme	• Purchase equipment
Training (Peter)			• 1st draft training plan	• 2nd draft training plan • Research more formal courses • Recruit volunteer team	• Initial training programme	• **FINAL STAFF & VOLUNTEER TRAINING**
Venue (Sue)	• Research venues available • Produce costings	• Produce plans according to activities required	• Recruit decorators	• Choose venue – secure rental agreement • Plan decoration phases	• 1st phase decoration	• 2nd phase decoration • Purchase equipment

Table 2 (*continued*)

CPA

OBJECTIVE	OCT 02	NOV 02	DEC 02	JAN 03	FEB 03	MAR 03
Communicating with the church (Dave)	• Ongoing communication	• Invites to launch				↑
External partnerships (Hannah)	• Ongoing communication					↑
Funding (Sarah)	• Plans for year 2					↑
Marketing (Becca)	• Invitations sent to press, local dignataries and other key people	• Press release drafted • Advertising placed	• Invitations followed up • Final logistics organised	• LAUNCH PROJECT		
Programme (John)	• FINAL PROGRAMME OF EVENTS AGREED	• Brainstorming of new ideas		↑		
Training (Peter)	• Plan next level of training		↑			
Venue (Sue)	• 3rd phase of decoration	• 4th phase of decoration	• VENUE OPERATIONAL			

Recording the detail

- Once you have your overall CPA, you will need to detail each month's activity in the form of weekly schedules, which can be expressed in a listing style. (See Table 3.)

- Each week will take you progressively closer to your end objective.

- You should record two months ahead only, as this level of detail will change fairly frequently.

- Re-evaluate the tasks to do each week. This will help you to check when things are likely to fall behind. Make sure team members notify the team leader/manager when they know this is likely to happen, as it may affect other areas of responsibility.

KEY POINT: Copy all three sets of records – the overall picture, the monthly CPA and the weekly schedule – to the whole team.

Table 3

WEEKLY SCHEDULE
Week beginning 1st April 02

OBJECTIVE	TASK	MEANS OF ACHIEVEMENT	PEOPLE INVOLVED/ LEAD PERSON	DATE REQUIRED FOR COMPLETION
Communicating with the church	1st draft of proposal to give to the church	Whole team to submit their sections to lead person	All team, led by Dave	Fri 5th April
External partnerships	Arrange meeting to discuss who we should target	Diaries to be co-ordinated	All team, led by Hannah	Wed 3rd April
Funding	Begin research of trusts, local businesses, etc. 1st draft of letter to send	Gather directories, yellow pages, local newspapers Write it	Sarah	Fri 5th April
Marketing	NO ACTIVITY	————————→		
Programme	Begin research for ideas	Other local projects, national youth organisations	John	Fri 5th April
Training	NO ACTIVITY	————————→		
Venue	Research venues available Produce Budgets	Local newspapers, local estate agents, church buildings Itemise key expenditure and research likely costs	Sue	Fri 5th April

There should be four or five of these each month, each one building on the
previous week's activities until the month's goals are achieved.

4.5: Why Evaluate?

Monitoring is the regular and ongoing task of checking where you are in relation to fulfilling your project's aims and objectives (see 4.3: The Strategy Wheel). An evaluation is a major review, reassessment or analysis of where you are going and what impact your project is having.

An effective evaluation process will enable you to:

- ensure you are meeting your aims and objectives;
- recognise your successes;
- learn from your mistakes;
- identify future opportunities;
- prioritise your resources;
- implement changes;
- improve your quality of service;
- raise your standards;
- inform your decisions about future work;
- understand what makes a difference to your users;
- set realistic targets for the way ahead;

- report to funders;
- build future funding applications.

You may wish to carry out a full evaluation at the end of the first year and perhaps every couple of years following that. However, remember that it takes time for a project to make an impact and that the results of preventative work in particular can be difficult to show in the short term.

How to evaluate

It is possible to buy in outside consultancy to carry out an evaluation. This has its pros and cons. Outside evaluation is perhaps a little more objective, but on the other hand can lack an understanding of some of your specific issues and pressures. Consultants can also prove expensive and most projects will find that a process of self-evaluation is well within their means and acceptable to their funders.

Five steps to implementing an effective evaluation:
1. Identify how you will measure whether your project is making a difference.
2. Decide what information you need to gather.
3. Plan how you will collect this information.
4. Evaluate the information.
5. Use the results.

Step 1: How will we measure whether we are making a difference?

In order to establish whether your aims and objectives are being achieved you will need to develop some measures of success, or what are known as *performance indicators*. Performance indicators are like road signs that allow you to see whether you're on the right track, how far you have travelled and how far you still have to go to reach your destination.

Performance indicators can be:

- *Quantitative* – i.e. 'hard data' statistics (see 3.3: Gathering Information). For example, how many people use your project? How often do they use it? How long do they use it for?

- *Qualitative* – i.e. 'soft data' (view points, opinions, comments, etc., see 3.3: Gathering Information). 'I feel 100 per cent better than I did', 'They always have time to listen', 'I've got a new confidence about money', etc.

To build an accurate picture of your project's effectiveness you must use both quantitative and qualitative performance indicators. Simply measuring the number of people using your service will not, on its own, tell you whether your service is meeting the identified need. As well as counting the quantity of people using a service, it is vital to measure its quality through the use of questions put to users about their experience.

Step 2: What information do we need to collect?

Think through a number of qualitative and quantitative performance indicators for each of your strategic aims and objectives. Because they are SMART (i.e. Specific, Measurable, Attainable, Relevant and Time-specific) this should be easy to do. In fact, if you can't, it's time to rethink your objectives. Why not ask your project users what kind of indicators they think should be used to measure the project's success? You might find this enlightening in and of itself!

Step 3: How will we collect the information?

It is essential to assess what all the stakeholders in your project think about the work you do. These will include your service users, people who refer others to your project, other organisations you work with, your staff and volunteers. Select appropriate methods of collecting both quantitative and qualitative data. These could include:

● questionnaires;
● interviews;
● focus groups;
● comments and suggestions boxes or books;
● a graffiti wall.

(For more on the above see 3.5: A Five-step Research Plan.)

Step 4: Evaluating the information

Look again at the relevant results of the community research you carried out before setting up your project (see Section 3: Researching Your Community). Compare these with the results you have just obtained from Step 3. The changes that have taken place may be attributed to the impact of your project.

Note, however, that other factors may also have contributed to changes in your area. Though time consuming, the way to isolate the changes that can be specifically credited to your project is to carry out what is known as a 'baseline' study before you set up your project. Here you compare your proposed 'project' community with another similar community where you will not be working (known as a 'control' community). Then, as part of your evaluation, you look at the changes in your 'project' area and compare them with the situation in the control community. The differences can be attributed to the impact of your project.

Step 5: Using the results

Put the results of your evaluation into a written report (see 3.6: Analysing Your Data). If you decide to opt for in-house evaluation, it is worthwhile sending an appropriate team member on a relevant training course. Contact your local Council for Voluntary Services (CVS) or Voluntary Sector Officer at the Local Authority or the Charities Evaluation Services to find out details of what is available (see below).

If you are overly critical the effect will be de-motivating for everybody concerned. If you're uncritically positive there will be missed opportunities for improvement. Be careful that it does not undermine workers' or users' confidence in themselves or the organisation, but neither leave them complacent about the future. Be honest yet balanced.

RESOURCES AND CONTACTS

The Charities Evaluation Services (CES)
4 Coldbath Square
London EC1R 5HL
Tel: 020 7717 5722
Website: www.ces.vol.org.uk
Training, advice and information on monitoring and evaluation, and quality assurance systems for the voluntary sector.

Further reading

Managing Evaluation by Willem Van Der Eyken (Charities Evaluation Services).

Managing Quality of Service by Alan Lawrie (Directory of Social Change, 1995).

Monitoring Ourselves by Anne Connor (Charities Evaluation Services).

Partnerships for Learning – A guide to evaluating arts projects by Felicity Woolf (Arts Council of England).

4.6: Financial Planning

The importance of financial planning

All projects begin with a vision rather than a balance sheet. It is the way it's meant to be. As Proverbs 29:18 explains, 'Where there is no vision, the people perish.' And as the Bible shows us time and again, resources follow vision not vice versa. Financial planning, however, is still an absolute necessity if a vision is going to become a healthy reality and achieve any long-term sustainability. Too many well-intentioned (and badly needed) projects have collapsed because insufficient attention was paid to how the figures stacked up. And no project can operate on thin air alone!

While financial planning is essential, it need not be as complicated as many people would have you believe. Of course, if you can it's a good idea to find someone with a financial background to be part of the project planning team (see 4.2: The Project Team) but, in reality, from the moment we first receive pocket money we all begin setting budgets, establishing cash-flow forecasts and identifying cost centres – we work out how much we can afford within our means, we work out how long we can make our money last, and we work out the kinds of things we might spend it on. In other words, don't worry – financial planning is not beyond you. By following a series of four straightforward steps you can soon produce the financial information you need.

Step 1: Identifying the type of financial information you might need

There are various ways of presenting financial information in order to demonstrate different issues. Some of the main types are listed below:

- *A budget* – a forecast or estimate of income and expenditure during a set period, perhaps a month or a year: what's likely to come in versus what's likely to have to be spent.

- *A cash-flow forecast* – a timed forecast of when money will be coming in compared with when it will be spent.

- *A balance sheet* – a 'snapshot' list of the assets and liabilities of the project at any one point in time: what it owns versus what it owes.

- *An income and expenditure account* – an historical record of what payments were received and what payments were paid out during a given period, including money owed to and owed by the project.

It is likely that projects will need all of these types of information at some point during their lifetime.

- If a project is looking for sources of funding it is unlikely that any potential donor will part with their money without seeing some form of *budget*. The more a project needs, the more detailed the information it is likely to have to give.

● If a project is seasonal, or if it has irregular sources of funding, a *cash-flow forecast* is essential to make sure that at no point will the project run out of money – even if only temporarily – and prevent it from carrying out its activities.

● At any one point in time a project should be able to assess its exact financial situation as a basis from which it can plan ahead. To do this it will need to draw up a *balance sheet*.

● If the project is a charitable organisation, or part of a charitable organisation, it will need to produce *income and expenditure accounts* or a Statement of Financial Activities (SOFA) in accordance with Charity Commission guidelines.

ACTION: If you are thinking about starting a new project it is likely that the piece of financial information you need most urgently is a project budget. The following steps will focus on how to develop a project budget.

Step 2: Working out how much your project will cost

It is often difficult to estimate how much a project will cost before it has even begun. For a start, you might not be able to be sure about levels of demand – how many people might use the project – and whether people using it would be prepared to pay anything towards its costs. One of the best ways to assess such information is to speak with people running similar projects to find out how they estimate their costs and then base your assumptions on the information they supply.

Costs can also be broken down into two types:

- *Capital costs* – those things that you buy once, normally at the beginning of the project, and continue to use throughout its lifetime. This might include things like computers, other office equipment, furniture, a vehicle, machinery and perhaps even a building.

- *Revenue costs* – those payments that are made on a regular basis and recur for as long as the project keeps going. These are many and various, as set out in Table 4.

Estimating how much certain things will cost is only part of the problem though. One of the most difficult challenges in setting a project budget is making sure you don't forget anything. In order to make sure nothing is forgotten try using the checklist on the next page.

Table 4

Costs	Notes	Cost	Total cost
Capital costs			
Buildings	Construction, purchase, refurbishment, professional fees but NOT rent.		
Vehicles	Van, minibus, car, etc.		
Office equipment	Computers, printers, fax machine, telephones but NOT general stationery.		
Furniture	Office furniture, armchairs, beds, etc.		
Total capital costs			
Revenue costs		**Cost** per unit (per person, per year, per visit, per session, etc.)	
Salaries	Most projects use standard pay scales – the local authority, CVS or church denomination should have information to help setting rates (see 5.9: Employing Staff).		
National Insurance	Currently 11.9 per cent on earnings above £4,535 per annum.		
Pensions	This will be a matter for the project to decide, but it is important that there is a clear policy that applies to all employees (see 5.9: Employing Staff).		
Recruitment	Advertisements in appropriate papers, websites. Expenses paid to interviewees. Mailouts to applicants, etc.		

Table 4 *(continued)*

Costs	Notes	Cost	Total cost
Payroll charge	Many projects use the payroll system of another organisation to pay staff. This sometimes has a charge.		
Rent and rates	Excluding heating, lighting, etc.		
Running costs	Includes heating, lighting, stationery, telephone, postage, day-to-day petty cash, photocopying, etc. Often includes any small payments not listed elsewhere. (May be worth breaking this down further.)		
Producing information	Project flyers, brochure, annual report or other reports. Big photocopying jobs, posters, etc. (can include design costs).		
Fees for freelance workers/ consultants	Very often it is helpful for a project to hire in an 'expert' to help with a particular piece of work, e.g. setting up a website, carrying out an audit.		
Travel for staff and volunteers	It is important to have a policy in place setting out acceptable forms of transport, mileage rates, the need for receipts, etc.		
Training for staff and volunteers	Everybody will have some training needs. This could be for courses, books or for a regular mentor to support a worker.		
Specific project costs	Every project will have its own particular costs, such as raw materials, special meeting expenses, training.		
Contingency	It is good to set a contingency in case things don't go to plan and to allow some scope to develop new ideas.		

Table 4 *(continued)*

Costs	Notes	Cost	Total cost
Evaluation/ development	It may cost something to get project users involved in evaluating the project or hiring an independent consultant to help (see 4.5: Why Evaluate?).		
Replacement/ repair	Capital items will have a limited life expectancy and so it is important to build in a cost for repair/replacement.		
Insurance	(Self-explanatory)		
Bank charges/ interest	If you predict cash-flow problems or the need to borrow money, this must be budgeted for.		
Total revenue costs			
TOTAL COSTS			

Larger organisations may find it difficult to apportion all of their costs to a particular project. For example, a church administrator may be shared between the church and two community projects. These costs are known as 'indirect' or 'core' costs as they are not directly associated with any one project. Because many funders are reluctant to directly fund such costs it is important to develop what is known as a 'cost-centred budget'. Rather than separate out an indirect cost it is better to work out how much of it might be associated with your project and then include it as part of the project budget. For example, if the church administrator spends one-third of his or her time on your project work, then one-third of his or her salary costs should be built into your budget. A large organisation with several projects will develop a series of 'cost centres', and each one will be charged a proportion of 'core' or indirect costs.

ACTION: Go through the table above with your working group and estimate how much the costs will be for the first year of your project. Repeat the exercise for two years. This information will be vital both for the project and for any potential funders or investors.

Step 3: Identifying sources of income

Once you have worked out how much your project is going to cost to run, the next question is to work out where the money is going to come from. There are many potential sources of income. It very much depends on the nature of your project as to the sources you will be able to draw on. A community café, for example, is likely to be able to generate a fair amount of its income simply from the sale of cups of tea and coffee or other goods. An educational project for the benefit of homeless young people will be less able to generate its own income and will be more dependent on different forms of grant. Table 5 attempts to set out some of the different types of income that a project could draw on.

Try to develop a good balance between different sources of income so that you don't end up trusting all your eggs to one basket. Naturally many projects are established on the basis of a single grant, with little consideration of other forms of future income. However, this is dangerous because when the initial grant comes to an end, it is often too late to seek new forms of income at that stage. As a result the project may be forced to close, particularly when many funders do not allow subsequent applications to be made for additional grants.

Table 5

Source of income	Notes	Income per unit (per person, per year, per visit, per session, etc).	Total income
Grants	From statutory bodies such as the local authority, health authority, national government, etc. From grant-making trusts or companies. (See 5.2: Identifying Potential Funders.)		
Income from services/service users	Service users may pay a charge for the service they receive or for something they buy. This might also include rent if you are sharing a building, or the hire of certain resources belonging to the project.		
Service agreements and fees	Some projects have contracts with a local authority or public agency to provide certain services. Others may charge a consultancy or management fee to undertake an activity or project.		
Donations and subscriptions	Gifts received from public fundraising, sponsorships and legacies or subscriptions if the project has some form of membership scheme.		
Investment income	Interest/dividends received if the project is fortunate enough to have some form of endowment set aside.		
Total income			

Think about trends in income. For example, recent changes in legislation concerning refugees and asylum seekers may mean that there will be fewer grants and contracts for projects dealing with 'dispersal' issues, as the new policy seeks to centralise services provided to such people. Or falling revenues for the National Lottery may mean smaller, or more targeted, Community Fund Grants. Any good budget will assess the likely income trends and plan accordingly.

ACTION: Again, work through the table with your group. You may need to go away and do some further research into funding sources to gain a clearer idea of how much you might expect from certain trusts or statutory agencies. You may need to do some market research. But remember to make sure you work on a number of potential sources and build these plans into the wider action plan for the project.

Step 4: Setting a project budget and cash-flow forecast

Having gathered all of your information about predicted costs and potential sources of income, there is a simple question to ask: Will our estimated income cover our estimated costs?

Of course, in reality it's never quite as straightforward as that. We adjust our figures up and down to make them balance, or in some cases to make a profit. We try to assess how we could attract a few more users to bump up our income or how we could cut down on costs to make ends meet. However, too much fiddling with the figures is dangerous: over-ambitious income targets can put a project on an insecure footing (and will soon be spotted by a funder), while too much scrimping and scraping could make it impossible to deliver a quality service and jeopardise the project from the users' point of view. Sometimes it is more sensible to go back to the project objectives and slim things down or change emphasis to make the whole thing more realistic and achievable. This can mean placing more focus on those things that either cost less or generate more income, or sometimes it can mean putting a slightly different spin on things to become more funder-friendly!

Whatever means you use to get your figures to balance (or ideally make an operating profit), your project budget will simply comprise a table for expenditure (costs) over a fixed period of time and a table for income (over the same period of time). This will become the basis on which actual income and expenditure can be measured and an assessment made as to whether reality is keeping up with the projections your group made.

At this point it is also useful to work out when it is likely that money will flow in and out of the project: a cash-flow forecast. This is most easily done by taking the different categories set out in your project budget tables and writing them down the left-hand side of the page and then writing the months of the year across the top of the page. In each month write down how much it is likely you will spend or receive out of each category. You can then add the total income and expenditure for each month of the year, subtract one from the other and make an assessment as to whether there will be enough money in the bank in each month for your various costs to be met. Where necessary, finances will need to be sought up front or borrowed in order that the project can remain solvent from one month to the next.

ACTION: Take the income and expenditure tables you have already produced and work them together into a project budget, making alterations as necessary to ensure they balance. Ask yourselves whether this looks like a viable project. Then imagine you had a large sum of money to invest. Would you be prepared to invest it on the basis of the figures you have set out?

Also produce the monthly cash-flow table as described above. Can you foresee which months are most likely to put pressure on project finances? Can you think of a way around such difficult months (e.g. making sure people pay swiftly, delaying paying bills, spreading out expenditure into instalments, taking out loans, etc.)?

Accountancy

Maintaining up-to-date accounts is not only good practice from the public accountability point of view, it is also necessary to help you make the right decisions on how your project needs to develop in the future.

Get a copy of 'Accounting and Reporting by Charities: Statement of Recommended Practice' issued by the Charity Commission. The SORP (as it is known) sets out recommendations on the standards a charity should adopt in reporting on the resources entrusted to it and the activities it undertakes. And even if you are not setting up a charity for your project, it is still good to follow generally accepted standards of best practice.

The amount of information you need to make publicly available, and whether that information will need to be audited annually by an independent accountant, depends on the size (in financial terms) of your activities. In the first few years it is unlikely that you will need to produce anything more than simple receipt and payment accounts, together with a list of your assets. However, as you reach and pass the turnover thresholds set out in the SORP, it will become necessary to involve someone with professional financial skills in your management group to help you with these aspects of running your project.

KEY SOURCE: *The Complete Guide to Business and Strategic Planning* (2nd edn) by Alan Lawrie (Directory of Social Change, 2001).

4.7: Business Plans

What is a business plan?

All the hard work is done. You have your vision. You've clarified your mission. You've identified your key partners. You've set up a project team. You've worked out aims, objectives and key tasks. You know who will be doing what. You know how you're going to keep records and monitor your progress. Your financial plan is in place. So what do you do next? You write it all down and turn it into a business plan!

Developing a business plan can sound tedious. But the truth is that you have already done most of the hard work, and putting it into a business plan will be a great asset.

A business plan operates at two levels:

A project road map

As an internal document your business plan becomes the road map for your project. It sets out the intended journey for staff and volunteers, but at the same time helps the project assess when it has strayed off course and needs to steer back on track. Of course, the vision for a project must never become constrained by the plan, and in that sense it is important that the plan is reviewed and revised every few years, but at the same time it does offer a benchmark for all activities to be measured against. It asks the question at any point in time: Is this what we set out to do?

A project PR tool

As an external document your business plan can be used to sell your project to potential funders and investors. A good business plan will give any interested party an idea of what your project is all about, as well as reassure them that it has been well thought through and has a sustainable future. Many funders now require a business plan before they will even consider making a grant.

Because the business plan can be used for different purposes it is increasingly common to find that projects have one core business plan for the use of key staff, and a series of summarised or amended versions:

- An executive summary, setting out a brief outline of the project, its aims, context and proposed direction (normally no more than two pages).
- A summary public document, setting out all the main points in a more 'glossy' format to be used more as a marketing tool (no more than six pages).
- An action plan for internal use, focusing on some of the key targets and activities.

The key elements of a good business plan

Table 6 below sets out some of the key elements of a good business plan. It suggests a particular order for each element, although it very much depends on each plan as to exactly what is most appropriate.

Top tips for writing a good business plan

- Keep it simple. Most people are unlikely to read more than 20 pages at a time without the main direction being lost. Avoid jargon.

- Make no assumptions. Do not expect people to understand what your project is about. Make it crystal clear what the needs of the users are and how they will benefit from your work.

- Give it some oomph. Use summaries and action points to give your plan a sense of purpose and direction. Be bold and task-centred – avoid terms like 'We hope to. . .' and say things like 'We will. . .' instead!

- Demonstrate some of your own reflection and analysis, as well as that of the users (see 4.3: The Strategy Wheel), to show that you have thought this through and it is not simply a rushed funding bid. Use graphs, charts and tables to set out thinking as clearly as possible.

- Get somebody else who knows little or nothing about the project to read your plan in order to identify any sections that are not as clear as they might be.

Table 6

Section	Content
Contents	Simple list of contents.
Executive summary	Brief outline of your overall vision, values and the need you want to meet.
Introduction and mission	The project mission statement/aim, with an explanation of the purpose and duration of the plan.
Organisation background and track record	A brief review of the project/organisation and its activities to date, showing strengths and achievements. Include legal status, scale and size.
Needs/trends analysis	Outline of the current context – may draw from audit information and/or the expressed needs of potential users. Demonstrate your awareness of the broader national policy context and other external developments.
Strategic aims/Objectives	Statement of your aims and objectives, together with some indication as to what assumptions underpin the project and the main direction and priorities of those involved.
Key tasks/targets (action plan)	Demonstrate how each objective will be achieved through a series of key timed tasks, each with a measurable target and/or outcome.
Management and staffing	Set out the management and staffing implications for the direction of work. Make the case that the project has the necessary competencies to manage the plan. This may include short biographies of staff and management committee.
Financial planning	The project budget – income and expenditure projections, including the basis upon which they are being made, e.g. how costs are estimated, justification for pricing policy, fundraising strategy, etc. Also include cash-flow forecast.
Monitoring and evaluation	Set out how the project will be monitored and records will be kept. May also set out how users will be involved in this process.
Immediate action plan	Set out some of the key immediate action steps, including dates for completion and people responsible.
Contact details	Details of the key contact: address, email, website, etc.

- Make sure there is a good balance between broad strategy and detail. Readers will not want a very abstract read, but at the same time they need to be caught by the vision, not bogged down in detail.

- Involve colleagues and users in drafting ideas to ensure they have some ownership in the document.

- Make sure it becomes a working document. Keep it handy in the office so that people can refer to it whenever they feel a need for clarity or inspiration.

- Monitor the plan and assess the extent to which its objectives are being met and its assumptions upheld.

KEY SOURCE: *The Complete Guide to Business and Strategic Planning* (2nd edn) by Alan Lawrie (Directory of Social Change, 2001).

SECTION 5:

How to Implement Your Project

5.1: Forming a Management Committee

Why a management committee?

As your project progresses it will become important that your informal project team transforms itself into a formal management committee.

Your church will very probably already be a registered charity, in which case it will have an official governing management body or executive in place. (There are many titles that can be given to such a body, e.g. Church Council, eldership, diaconate, etc.) If this is the case it will be appropriate to appoint what is in effect a sub-committee, accountable to your church's main management committee, to take delegated responsibility for your project.

Alternatively, you may decide to set up an independent charity. It might prove to be the right route forward if your project is a joint church initiative, if it will have a substantial budget in relation to your church's existing annual turnover, or if the church does not feel it can take responsibility for your project for other reasons. (In this case, see 5.3: Setting up a Charity.)

The purpose of a management committee

The purpose of a management committee is to report and hold itself accountable to the church's governing body and specifically fulfil the following tasks on their behalf:

● Determine the project's mission and purpose.

● Develop and agree the project's strategic/long-term plan.

● Develop and agree the project's policies.

● Ensure the project's resources (property, money, land, etc.) are accounted for, protected and managed effectively.

● Ensure the project has adequate resources.

● Establish procedures for recruiting, employing and supporting members of staff.

Operating your management committee

Decide at the outset how your management committee will operate. You will obviously need to present your thinking in the form of recommendations to the main governing body of your church for their approval.

Answer the following questions:

● Who will make up the group? Which categories should membership be drawn from in order to retain appropriate representation from involved parties?

● Who will chair the meetings? The chair of the committee should be appointed from among the members.

- What will be the length of service for its members and the period of time before re-election?
- What will be the frequency and timing of meetings?

5.2: Identifying Potential Funders

Developing a funding strategy

Here are four key points:

1. Many projects start with the promise of funding from a single source, which may be sufficient to get it up and running. However, as the work develops you will soon need to identify other sources of funding in order to meet the ongoing expenditure and provide for a sustainable future. It's always vital to avoid relying too heavily on one funding source in order to build sustainability. If a project is over-reliant on a single source of finance which then dries up, it will become vulnerable and with insufficient time to raise alternative funding will inevitably fold. Always remember that it's difficult to raise money in a crisis situation; generally, people like to put their money into going concerns!

2. Your ongoing funding strategy must allow for the varying and often lengthy timescales built into application processes. Few funders are able to give an immediate response to a request. The majority of applications will take

several months (sometimes up to a year) between the point of initial application and finally receiving the go-ahead.

3. The majority of secular funders will not fund 'religious' activity, which means that you need to be very clear that your project is meeting a welfare/social need and is not a vehicle for proselytism or primarily an in-house activity for church members if you are planning to approach them for help.

4. Most potential funders will only give to registered charities. However, if your project is not a charity in its own right but is under the authority of a local council this will, in most cases, be sufficient.

Main funding sources

Charitable trusts

These may be local or national. Useful publications to start your search include *A Guide to the Major Trusts* and a series of *Guides to Local Trusts*, available in the reference section of your local library. Also, for Lions, Rotary, etc., see your local Yellow Pages.

Media grants (e.g. Comic Relief, BBC Children in Need)

Contact them directly for details of criteria and deadlines for applications.

Statutory funding

Contact your local council for details of government grant initiatives that apply to your area, such as Single Regeneration Budget (SRB) (see 5.11: Working with Local Government).

Local government contracts

Local governments increasingly offer contracts to the voluntary sector agencies to deliver certain services (see 5.11: Working with Local Government).

Community Fund (formerly National Lotteries Charities Board)

Many churches and Christian groups will not wish to apply for this funding on ethical grounds, so it is important that any decision is fully discussed and agreed by the offical management body before the application is made. Contact the Lotteries Board directly for details about the current programmes.

Companies and businesses

Many local or national businesses have a community affairs department (though that may not be what it is called), which funds charitable projects. Your nearest Chamber of Commerce may be able to give you information about businesses that support local causes and the relevant criteria.

In-house fundraising

This is money that you and your users raise through sponsored events, personal donations, standing orders, regular giving, etc.

Although initially attracting and then building this type of funding can seem like very hard work, it's an extremely useful resource for the following reasons:

- It often has no strings attached (officially what is known as 'unrestricted giving') and therefore can be used to fund areas of your work that are vital but may not be attractive to other funders (e.g. central administration, ongoing running costs). Funders often want to allocate the money they make available to specific aspects of your work (e.g. salaries, new equipment, new developments).

- It is an important and effective way of building a local support base while at the same time raising your profile locally.

- When regular, ongoing and, even better, given through a standing order, it helps create a solid underpinning and strength for your work.

Where to get advice

Contact the Council for Voluntary Service (CVS) or your local authority. A growing number of local authorities now have community fund officers. Find out who it is in your area and ask what advice they can give. Also ask about any training courses on offer.

There are also many good books available, but funding directories can be expensive and many are updated annually, so don't invest in your own copies. Instead contact your local Council for Voluntary Service or go to your local library.

Making an application

Each potential source of funding will have its own method of application, which you should check at the outset. Some have their own application forms, while others require you to write to them setting out your request in your own style.

Most have specific guidelines as to what projects they will fund. These often include:

- A user group (children, homeless people, people who are unemployed, etc.).
- A geographical area.
- A broad category of work (e.g. health, education).

Stick carefully within these guidelines. It is a waste of everybody's time to approach funders to give money outside of their stated field of interest.

Writing a letter of application

For funders that require you to write to them requesting money, your application should be:

- written on headed notepaper;
- addressed to a real person (phone to find out who);
- individually tailored to each funder's grant-making policy;
- clear, easily understood and without jargon;
- not patronising or presumptuous;
- no longer than two sides of A4.

It should contain the following information:

- Who you are.
- What you do.
- How you do it.
- When you do it.

- Who your project benefits.
- What has already been achieved.
- Your selling points (a few key reasons why your work is important and why donors will want to support you).
- The credibility of your organisation (which other organisations support or work with you, your membership of any relevant national or local bodies, etc.).
- An outline strategy and budget for your project, including which bits you are asking them to fund.
- Your business plan, if complete (see 4.7: Business Plans).

You should also be prepared to send your annual report if your organisation has been around for more than a year, your most recent accounts, your constitution (e.g. your latest evaluation), and any other information if requested.

Top tips for fundraisers

- Some aspects of your work will be easier to fund than others. Most funders like 'new' and 'finite' projects, which makes covering your ongoing running costs more difficult. Be prepared to review, refocus and repackage.
- Funders are always impressed if you can show that either you or another funder are already contributing towards the cost of what you are asking for. Your contribution does not have to be monetary, it can be in kind (e.g. x hours of staff/volunteers' time or x hours' rent of your premises).

- Whenever possible ask for funding for a number of years. If your funding is only agreed for a twelve-month period it tends to make life and long-term planning uncertain. Many funders will be open to a three-year funding application in the right circumstances.

- If your application is successful, always write and say thank you. Some funders have a procedure in place for you to report back at a specified time on how you spent their money and the difference that it made. If not, use your initiative. Keep in touch with regular updates on the progress of your project.

- Make sure that you appropriately acknowledge the support you have received. Discuss with the funder whether they would like you to display their logo on your literature, and, if so, how you should do this.

- Many funders have annual programmes of giving, so if you are unsuccessful on one occasion do not let it put you off reapplying for next year.

5.3: Setting up a Charity

Charities have special status and advantages under UK law. In return they are required to operate within a framework of supervision by the Charity Commission. A well-run charity is one that:

- achieves high standards and attracts public confidence and support;
- is set up with clearly documented aims and is run by committed people who manage and account for resources well;
- acts with integrity and without regard to the personal interests of its founders.

Advantages of setting up a charity

The main advantages of setting up a charity are that:

- it does not normally have to pay income tax, corporation tax or capital gains tax;

133

- stamp duty and gifts to a charity are free of inheritance tax;
- it does not normally pay more than 20 per cent of normal business rates on the buildings used to house it;
- it can get special VAT treatment in some circumstances.

The less tangible, but equally important, benefits of charitable status are that it is:

- much easier to raise funds from the public, local government and grant-making trusts when you have charitable status;
- the community is reassured to know that the activities of a charity are monitored by the Charity Commission;
- it can be easier to formally represent and help meet the needs of a community if you are a charity.

How to determine your charitable objectives

However, there are restrictions on what charities can do. A charity must have *exclusively* charitable purposes. If you are running an organisation that has a range of activities, some of which are not charitable, then you would have to stop those non-charitable activities in order to become a charity and would need to consider carefully whether or not charitable status is appropriate for you.

A charity's purposes are called its 'objects' and are set out in its governing document. There are four main charitable objects:

1. *The relief of financial hardship.* Hardship need not be long term. It could be short term, for example caused by loss of a job or sickness. Relief of hardship could be giving money, providing food, clothing or housing, by giving advisory or other services to those in need.

2. *The advancement of education.* This is not limited to formal education such as schools and universities, but includes setting up playgroups or providing work-related training.

3. *The advancement of religion.* No distinction is made between one religion and another since there is a general assumption that religion is for the public benefit.

4. *Certain other purposes for the benefit of the community.* These are:

   ● The relief of old age, sickness or disability.

   ● Promoting racial harmony.

   ● The resettlement and rehabilitation of drug users and offenders.

   ● The provision of recreational facilities that are open to everyone.

   ● Promoting industry and business for the benefit of the public.

On top of this, a key criterion for establishing a charity under any of the objects listed above is that the charity is for the *public benefit*. A charity must benefit the community and not simply those who set it up, such as its trustees or employees.

Urban and rural regeneration

The Charity Commissioners have now recognised the promotion of urban and rural regeneration for the public in areas of social and economic deprivation as being a charitable purpose in its own right. This is not, strictly speaking, a fifth charitable 'object', as the purpose of such a charity still has to fall within the four objects listed above. Organisations may achieve the charitable purpose of urban and rural regeneration by doing some or all of the following:

- Provide financial or other assistance to people who are poor.
- Provide housing for those in need and help to improve housing standards generally in those parts of an area of deprivation where poor housing is a problem.
- Provide public amenities.
- Provide education, training and retraining opportunities and work experience, especially for unemployed people.
- Provide financial or technical assistance or advice to new businesses or existing businesses where it would lead to training and employment opportunities for unemployed people.
- Provide, maintain and improve roads and accessibility to main transport routes.
- Provide, maintain and improve recreational facilities.
- Preserve buildings in the area which are of historic or architectural importance.

- Provide land and buildings on favourable terms to businesses in order to create training and employment opportunities for unemployed people.
- Help unemployed people find employment.

In order to be a charity, a regeneration organisation will need to demonstrate that the geographical area in which it works is in need of regeneration. This can be done by setting out objective criteria against which the area's needs are assessed:

- Be involved in at least three or four of the activities listed above, and show that these activities cover a broad spectrum of regeneration work.
- Show that the public benefit from its activities outweighs any private benefit that might be conferred on individuals or companies in the process of regenerating the community, for example help given to local businesses.
- Prove that its objects are exclusively charitable.

If you are interested in setting up a charity to promote urban and rural regeneration, contact the Charity Commission's registration staff on 0870 333 0123 and read their publication entitled *Promotion of Urban and Rural Regeneration RR2*.

Charities and trading

For those organisations intending to set up a charity that will engage in trading activities for fundraising purposes, it is important to determine whether or not a separate subsidiary trading company should be established to carry out those activities. The Commission's guidance note, *Charities and Trading CC35*, provides a useful starting point, but detailed information about the taxation of trading profits earned by charities should be obtained from the Inland Revenue, who have produced a comprehensive leaflet, *Trading by Charities (IR 2001)*, which can be viewed on their website: www.inlandrevenue.gov.uk.

Reform of the legal framework for the voluntary sector

There is currently a review being undertaken of the legal framework determining charitable status. This is because some aspects are viewed as outdated, particularly the need to fall within one of the four charitable objects listed on p.135. This review is currently being undertaken by a body called the Performance and Innovation Unit (PIU), which started work at the end of June 2001 under the supervision of Baroness Morgan and is due to report early in 2002. Information on the progress of the work of the PIU can be obtained from the Cabinet Office website at www.cabinet.office.gov.uk.

Appointing trustees

Trustees should be selected on the basis of their relevant skills and experience, and be prepared to take an active part in the running of the charity. They ought not to be appointed for their status or position in the community alone; this is the function of patrons.

Trustees can be personally liable for any breach of trust, for example if they enter into contracts in the course of administering the charity as a result of which they incur debts or liabilities that amount to more than the value of the charity's assets. In this case the charity's creditors may sue them personally for the difference.

Trustees:

- must be over the age of 18;
- cannot have any previous convictions for dishonesty;
- cannot be an undischarged bankrupt;
- cannot be previously disqualified as a company director.

More detailed information about the role and responsibilities of trustees is given in the *Charities Commission Publication CC3*.

Choosing a name

The name of a charity is important. It is this name that the public will remember most about a charity, therefore it should be sufficiently different from the names of other charities so as not to mislead them in any way. Before committing yourself to a particular name, for example by printing stationery or putting up sign-boards, check with the Charities Register to make sure that your proposed name is available and acceptable to them. You can do this either by viewing the Register of Charities Page on their website or by telephoning the Commission and asking for the Central Register. There is nothing stopping you putting up a sign-board with your chosen name before you have registered, but you cannot use the word 'charity' in that name until you have achieved registration.

Three kinds of charity

There are three main types of document that govern a charity. The type you choose will determine which type of organisation your charity will be. They are:

1. A constitution. This governs an unincorporated association.
2. A trust deed. This governs a trust.
3. Memorandum and Articles of Association. These govern a company limited by guarantee.

Table 7 outlines the type of organisation the various documents create, and what the advantages are of each organisational structure. However, it is not exhaustive. Consult the Charity Commission's publication *Choosing and Preparing a Governing Document CC22* for further information.

The Charity Law Association (CLA) produces suitable model documents (for which a charge will be made). The Charity Commission also produces model documents. Opting to adopt a model document will certainly speed up your application for registration.

Table 7

Governing document	Organisation created	Advantages	Disadvantages
Constitution • Trustees are usually called executive or management committee members. • Constitution is not a formal document and is put into operation by being 'adopted' at a formal meeting.	**Unincorporated association** • Suitable if organisation is to be relatively small in terms of assets and is to have a membership. • This structure may be appropriate for a community lunch club, a resource/ information centre, a residents' association.	• Flexibility – can get project off the ground quickly. • No statutory controls. • Easy to set up and run – no need for legal help in drafting constitution. • Financial autonomy.	• Not a company, therefore unable to own land or investments, or enter into contracts or employ people in its own name. • No limited liability – trustees may be liable for repayments of debts.
Trust deed • A trust is run by trustees. • A trust deed is a formal document and you may need legal advice to complete and execute it. • Once a trust deed has been executed, it should be sent to the Inland Revenue Office of the Controller of Stamps in case it attracts stamp duty. Check with the Stamp Office: 020 7438 7452.	**Trust** • Suitable if organisation is to be run by a small group of people and is not going to rely on a membership for any part of its administration. • A trust may be helpful if a large sum of money has been given for a specific purpose or if you want to help a particular group of people by receiving and distributing donations.	• Trustees only answerable to Charity Commission, therefore no outside bodies can interfere in business of trust. • Relatively cheap to set up – no registration fees. • Trustees make all the decisions – no need to call members together.	• A trust cannot own land or sign documents in its own name – assets must be put in name of trustees. • Difficult to challenge the decisions of trustees or remove trustees. • Difficult to alter a trust deed. • Trustees personally liable for trust's debts.
Memorandum and Articles of Association • Trustees are called board, council of management or directors. • Subject to company law and therefore can be quite complex – will need legal adviser to set up. Contact Companies House at Cardiff CF4 3UZ: 02920 380801.	**Company limited by guarantee** • Suitable if the organisation is quite large, will employ a lot of staff, will regularly enter into commercial contracts, will be a substantial owner of property. • Examples where this type of organisation may be appropriate: a training organisation or the development of a site for a range of community activities.	• Incorporated, so can own land, employ people, enter into contracts. • Limited liability, so directors not *normally* liable personally for debts. • Members have control to elect directors and hold them to account.	• Company must ensure that it complies with company law and charitable law. Accounts and other documents must be filed annually in the appropriate format at the time required. • A more expensive structure to maintain – annual fee involved in the preparation and audit of accounts. • Documentation filed with the Registrar of Companies is available for public scrutiny.

Registering a charity

To register a charity you will need to do the following:

- Ask the Charity Commission to send you their pack containing an application form (APP1) and a declaration form (DEC1).

- Ensure that application is completed by all trustees.

- Submit any relevant supporting information that will help the Commission understand exactly how your organisation will meet its charitable aims. For example, if your organisation intends to work with children or young people, the Commission may carry out checks with other governmental departments and statutory bodies, as well as any other organisations mentioned in the application. It is important to give as much information as possible. Include any promotional literature, independent assessments from experts, newspaper articles and so on.

In general, the Commission will reply to your application within 15 working days of receipt. They will not normally consider an application where the governing document is in draft form, or if the organisation does not yet exist. The reason for this is that, in their experience, organisations that already exist have a clear idea of the way in which they will carry out their objects, whereas organisations submitting a draft document are never actually set up. The main thing the Commission will look at is whether the proposed activities are exclusively charitable. If your application is successful, the date of registration will be the date on which the Commission enters your organisation on the register of charities.

All charities must register unless they fall within one of the exempt categories. These charities include those that have an income of less than £1,000 per year and do not own or occupy any land or buildings and do not have a permanent endowment.

A frequently asked question by those who want to register their organisation as a charity in the form of a company limited by guarantee is: What is the best way of going about this? Before trying to register as a charitable company, you must do the following:

- Contact Companies House.
- Obtain registration by Companies House of your organisation as a company limited by guarantee.
- Wait to receive your Certificate of Incorporation from Companies House.
- Contact the Charity Commission and ask to be sent a registration pack.

However, there is just one quirk. Any proposed company that wants to use the word 'charity' or 'charitable' within their official name (e.g. St Augustine's Charitable Trust) first needs to send the agreed Memorandum and Articles to the Charity Commission and obtain a letter of approval before sending the document to Companies House for incorporation.

Charities, local authorities and contracts

County councils, district councils, London borough councils, the new unitary authorities and the Common Council of the City of London all have the power to keep a local index of charities and, with the trustees' consent, to review the work of that charity. The Charity Commission produces a publication, *Charities and Local Authorities* CC2, which describes the ways in which local authorities may be involved in how charities are run.

Increasingly, instead of receiving grants from public bodies, charities are being asked to enter into legally binding contracts with them to provide services on their behalf. If you are considering entering into such a contract, it is important that the contractual obligations are fully consistent with the objects of your charity. Otherwise you will be acting in breach of trust and your trustees could be personally liable for the performance of the contract – and for any damages payable if they do not fulfil the terms. It is recommended that you seek advice from the Charity Commission's support staff if you have any doubts about whether a proposed contract falls within your charity's objects.

Trustees cannot normally use a charity's funds to provide services that a public body is legally required to provide at the public expense. (However, trustees may use a charity's resources to supplement what the public body provides.) It is therefore important that charities do not enter into contracts to deliver a service that a public body is required to provide unless the public body pays the full economic cost.

For further advice on entering into contractual relationships with public funding bodies read the Charity Commission publication *Charities and Contracts CC37*. Other recommended reading is a publication produced by the National Council for Voluntary Organisations (NCVO) entitled *Mutual Obligations – NCVO's Guide to Contracts with Public Bodies*, which can be obtained from Hamilton House Mailings (tel: 01536 399 016). Community Matters is the umbrella body of the National Federation of Community Organisations and will provide advice on dealings with local authorities, including contracts (tel: 0207 226 0189).

RESOURCES AND CONTACTS

Charity Commission

The best source of information is to be found on the Charity Commission's website at www.charity-commission.gov.uk. All general telephone enquiries: 0870 3330123.

London
Harmsworth House
13–15 Bouverie Street
London EC4Y 8DP
Open 9am to 5pm weekdays

Liverpool
2nd Floor
20 Kings Parade
Queens Dock
Liverpool L3 4DQ
Open 9am to 5pm weekdays

Taunton
Woodfield House
Tangier
Taunton
Somerset TA1 4BL
Open 9am to 4pm weekdays

In relation to fundraising appeals, complex rules apply and you are advised to speak to the Charity Commission and seek guidance in their publication *Charities and Fundraising CC30*.

Other contacts

National Council for Voluntary Organisations (NCVO)
Regents Wharf
8 All Saints Street
London N1 9RL
Tel: 0800 2798 798
Purpose: Offers advice on a wide range of subjects, runs seminars and produces various publications (e.g. *The Good Trustee Guide*). To join the NCVO your organisation must be national or have the potential to become national. However, the Trustees Services Unit advice line can offer direct advice to local groups.

Directory of Social Change
24 Stephenson Way
London NW1 2DP
Tel: 020 7209 4949
Purpose: Offers a wide range of courses and training events on many subjects, including volunteer management,

communications and fundraising. Services available to any voluntary sector group.

Publications: *Guide to the Major Trusts* and *The Fund-raising Handbook*.

Charities Aid Foundation
25 Kingshill Avenue
Kings Hill
West Malling
Kent ME19 4TA
Tel: 01732 520000
Purpose: Gives advice to facilitate tax-efficient giving, and offers covenant administration services.

Action with Communities in Rural England (ACRE)
Somerford Court
Somerford Road
Cirencester
Gloucestershire GL7 1TW
Tel: 01285 653477
Purpose: Offers advice and support on a wide range of issues from registration to maintaining buildings. It also provides training and publishes books and leaflets and has a special service for the managing trustees of village halls called the National Village Halls Advisory Service.

Community Matters
1st Floor
12–20 Baron Street
London N1 9LL
Tel: 020 7837 7887
Fax: 020 7278 9253

Purpose: Provides advice and assistance, a community consultancy service, courses and a wide range of publications. Services are offered to new and established community organisations.

National Association of Councils for Voluntary Services (NACVS)
3rd Floor
Arundel Court
177 Arundel Street
Sheffield S1 2NU
Tel: 0114 278 6636
Purpose: The national umbrella body for 250 Councils for Voluntary Service in England. A local Council for Voluntary Service provides advice, support and information to voluntary organisations and charities in their area, including help with registration.

Interchange Legal Advisory Service
Interchange Studios
Hampstead Town Hall Centre
213 Haverstock Hill
London NW3 4QP
Fax: 020 7813 7493
Email: legal@interchange.org.uk
Purpose: Gives advice to charities on the preparation of governing documents, trust and charity law, and matters relating to trustees' responsibilities, employment, property, dissolution and insolvency.

Inland Revenue
Financial Intermediaries and Claims Office (FICO)
St John's House
Merton Road
Bootle
Merseyside L69 9BB
Tel: 0151 472 6000 (general switchboard)
      0151 472 6036/6037 (general enquiries – charities)
      0151 472 6038 (Gift Aid)
      0151 472 6043/6046 (charity trading)

Purpose: Responsible for meeting claims for repayment of tax on charity investment income and covenants. The Inland Revenue has a range of booklets about tax reliefs available to charities. Basic information on tax relief is given in leaflet *Inland Revenue 75, Tax Relief for Charities, Inland Revenue 113, Gift Aid: A Guide for Donors and Charities* and *CS2, Trading by Charities*.

Companies House
Cardiff CF4 3UZ
Tel: 0870 3333636
Purpose: The government agency that registers companies in the UK.

Housing Corporation
149 Tottenham Court Road
London W1P 6BN
Tel: 020 7393 2000
Purpose: Funds and regulates the housing associations in the UK, which manage around 1.5 million homes.

The London Stamp Office
The Controller of Stamps
Central Information Section
South West Wing
Bush House
London WC2B 4QN
Tel: 020 7438 7452
Purpose: The government agency in charge of administering stamp duty on legal documents.

The Charity Law Association
Ros Harwood
Rollit Farrel & Bladon
Rowntree Wharf
Navigation Road
York Y1 9WE
Fax: 01904 625807
Email: rjh@rollits.co.uk
Purpose: Assists with the legal apsects of registering as a charity.

5.4: Building a Team: How to Be Distinctively Christian

What are our distinctives?

There are many secular organisations today doing what churches and Christian organisations do – responding to social need, working in the community, etc. The distinguishing and distinctive feature of our work is our Christian faith. It is our faith that motivates us in the first place. Our faith remains the pivotal and fundamental aspect of all we do.

But if our faith makes us distinctive in our relationships with those we seek to serve, our faith must also make us different in the way we behave with each other.

We are relational. The apostle Paul described church as a body in which the parts relate to one another and are interdependent with one another. (We are known by our love for one another.) The way we treat one another in our work should make us as distinctive as the motivation for doing the work in the first place.

We believe in God-given potential. The recognition that we are all made in the image and likeness of God and all have

God-given potential is another key distinctive that sets Christian work apart from secular work. Secular organisations do not regard their human resources as God-given resources.

So how does our relational ethos and the recognition of our God-given potential get translated into our working practices?

Team-building

It's no statement of faith to acknowledge that Jesus of Nazareth remains the most influential leader ever to walk our planet. But read the opening few chapters of any of the Gospels, and you find a leader who was deeply committed to team-building.

Jesus understood that the success of his mission was in valuing, investing in and empowering others. Four soon became twelve, and twelve, seventy-two as he demonstrated his trust in his followers – something that did more for their self-esteem and owning of the mission than any fireside talk ever could.

However exceptional a visionary you are, if you can't build a committed, inspired and empowered team, whether it's made up of volunteers, employees or a mix of both, then you don't have a catalyst for change. Without a team of co-workers, any visionary's ability to achieve anything of lasting value will be very limited, and at the same time the vast pool of potential in their local church to deliver community transforming projects will remain untapped.

A great leader leaves you inspired by your own ability and potential rather than daunted by theirs. The hallmark of a truly great leader, therefore, is not so much what happens when they're around, but what happens when they're gone. 'Truly great leadership,' said Martin Luther King, 'is about what you achieve after you are dead.'

A strong team achieves the following:

- It provides the only effective means to achieve lasting goals and establish projects that will stand the test of time.
- It generates a high level of creativity and innovative ideas through the interaction of its members.
- It builds a diverse pool of talent and skills, which can be deployed to the best overall advantage.
- It increases its members' sense of involvement, belonging and commitment.
- It creates the environment to identify, train and enable future leaders.
- It develops the skills and potential of every member.

People before projects

John Adair breaks down the work of a team leader into three main areas:

- Achieving the task.
- Building and maintaining the team.
- Developing the individual.

No team should exist purely to fulfil a set of tasks. The reality is, however, that some leaders become so absorbed in getting the job done that they end up oblivious to the effects of their relentless pursuit on those who work with them. The human cost, in terms of quality of life and relationships, appears not to matter as long as the goal is achieved. But this attitude, often prevalent in business, industry and the voluntary sector, as well as in the church, is always shortsighted. Not only does it leave people drained of enthusiasm, feeling neglected, ignored and used, it eventually leaves them looking for a new job!

The members of your team are not just a means to an end; the bottom line is not simply about getting the job done, but also about enabling each individual to develop their full potential. Such concern will improve not only your relationships with them, but also their performance. 'Trust men and they will be true to you,' said Emerson. 'Treat them greatly and they will show themselves to be great.'

Choosing your team

'Human resources are the most critical part of any organisation's success. Good people help to ensure profitability, growth and long-term survival. You simply cannot survive without qualified people,' claims R. Maddux. So management experts suggest three key factors every leader should look for:

- Technical or professional competence.
- Ability to work as a team member.
- Desirable personal attributes and social skills.

However, as Phil Dobson, a local church leader in

Liverpool, puts it, 'You can be 98 per cent right and still 100 per cent wrong at the same time.' Or, to put it another way, in 1 Corinthians 1:26–27 Paul reminds his readers to 'think of what you were when you were called. Not many of you were wise by human standards; not many were influential; not many were of noble birth. But God chose the foolish things of the world to shame the wise; God chose the weak things of the world to shame the strong.'

Though the modern professional mind might find Paul's perspective absurd, the truth is that, despite all its problems, the church is without doubt the most successful organisation ever in terms of its growth and, of course, long-term survival. Jesus knew what it took to make a team work, but clearly did not believe this meant he had to restrict himself to those with proven ability. Instead, he could spot potential and was willing to invest in people, taking calculated risks in order to develop them.

Jesus saw what people could be: their undiscovered skills and abilities, not just their existing areas of competence (or incompetence!). Note his words to Simon in John 1:42: 'You are Simon son of John. You will be called Cephas' (which, as we know, is translated as 'Peter' or 'Rock'). All those who knew Simon knew that he could be impetuous and unreliable, and must have at least questioned Jesus' wisdom. Simon was more jelly-like than rock-like! Yet empowered by Jesus, Simon did eventually become Peter, the strong, dependable and wise founder member and leader of the church.

Modern business theory is geared towards playing safe. The majority of contemporary organisations and companies are run by people who are conservative by nature. But placing such high value on a proven track record, they lack the flexibility or courage to take risks and invest in latent potential. That's what makes Jesus' approach so different. Choosing team members on the basis of their latent potential will certainly involve taking risks, and not everyone will prove a diamond in the making. In truth, however, sometimes the most dubious raw material can yield surprising results if we are prepared to work hard and be patient.

With all this in mind, the following sections (5.5–5.9) are very important. They tackle the outworking of developing fair, consistent, transparent and accountable policies for working with volunteers and employees, which seek to put biblical theory into everyday practice.

5.5: Structuring Your Team

Before you start recruiting (either employees or volunteers) it's vital to think hard about the way in which you intend to structure your operation and therefore shape your team. Only then will you be in a position to make the right job choices. A huge temptation is to identify individual jobs, or even people to do jobs, before you have thoroughly thought through your whole operation. And the danger is that as a result you are likely to end up selling everyone short, which at best will cause confusion and at worst enormous difficulties in relationships and poor team morale.

Your team structure must follow the shape of your project rather than dictate it. If you put together a structure that does not reflect your proposed operation you are likely to end up with people doing jobs that don't really fit your needs or their skills. This is extremely common and will undoubtedly hinder your progress.

The key to getting your team structure right is being clear about the goals of your operation. However, having been round the Strategy Wheel (see 4.3: The Strategy

Wheel), you are in a good position to be able to think your operation through from beginning to end.

Identify groups of tasks

Put together tasks of a similar nature. As you do this, key elements of your operation will emerge. For example, if your project is a youth work project, the list of key elements might end up looking like this:

- Face-to-face youth work.
- Administration.
- Programme preparation.
- Premises/centre management.
- Team and project management (including budgeting and accounting).
- Fundraising.
- PR (Press Relations).
- Resourcing staff and volunteers.

Job structures

These groups of tasks will help you to begin to clarify a job and team structure.

- Sometimes one group of tasks constitutes a job, where-as at other times it is possible to bring several similar groups together to form a single job.
- Applying what information you have about the vol-ume and frequency of some of the tasks/groups of

tasks will begin to indicate how many hours a week are required for each job.

● You will then need to name the jobs, which will finally lead you on into the formation of the job description and person specification (see 5.9: Employing Staff).

● If your project involves development it might be that the structure of jobs in the early stages will be quite different from the structure required once it is established. If this is the case it will be important to design any contracts of employment you issue to reflect this. This might mean that some jobs are for a short term, with a specified end date. For instance, the person appointed to see through a development phase may not be the right person to manage the project long term. Development and management are very different tasks demanding very different skills.

● However you structure your team, ensure that there is a crystal clear management line. Who reports to whom? Why? Brainstorm this and then draw it up on a chart (see Figure 5) that explains the lines of accountability.

Figure 5

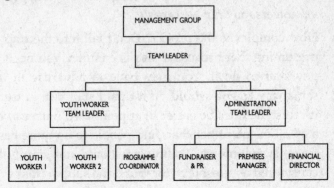

Volunteers or employees?

Once you have defined a draft team structure, consider how to resource it. Will it be staffed by paid workers, volunteers or a mixture of the two?

The temptation is to think that volunteers are only useful if you don't have the money to pay for staff. However, though lack of funds may well be a reason to involve volunteers, it should never be the only one. The decision to recruit paid staff or volunteers should always be a deliberate, conscious one.

The sorts of issues that affect how you resource your team structure may include the following:

- Is the project something that your local church or group of churches feels they 'own'? If they do, the structure may well be weighted to volunteers, particularly if there is a strong volunteer ethos in the church(es) and volunteering is promoted and taught as a part of Christian commitment.

- Is the project something your church is happy to support but too big or complex for them to 'own' as their operation? In which case finding a steady supply of volunteers may not be as easy.

- How complex is the project? Don't fall into the trap of presuming that because a task is complex you need to pay staff to do it. You may have to advertise in the same way as you would do for paid staff but, in truth, it can sometimes be easier to appoint a volunteer to do a complex job rather than find people to do more basic tasks as volunteers. Volunteers should not simply be considered as a resource for mundane support tasks.

5.6: Working with Volunteers

The last decade or so has seen an increased recognition of the role and potential of volunteers and interest in good management practices as they relate to them.

On a national basis the number of hours volunteers in faith-based projects contribute every week is huge.

- Active Christians and Jews are far more likely to be involved in community service than any other group. (Institute for Volunteering)

- The annual economic contribution of volunteers is around £500,000 per 100 community projects. (Shaftesbury – *Faith Makes Communities Work*)

- There are around 120,000 community projects run by churches in the UK, which means that volunteers contribute an estimated £600 million per year in time to Christian faith-based community projects. (Faithworks, 2001)

Bill Hybels famously makes the point that working with volunteers involves the purest form of leadership in the world. The reason is simple: employees will often endure bad leadership, put up with a lack of stimulation or cope with deep dissatisfaction for the money. A good pay packet covers a multitude of sins. But for volunteers no such monetary incentive exists. If their work is not fulfilling, they will vote with their feet. This means that volunteers need to be linked into your project in ways that are productive, that ensure they are valued, and that give them an opportunity to grow. And all this does not just happen. It needs careful planning.

Where to start

Think hard about establishing a set of clear policies or guidelines for working with volunteers. These will be based on the scale of your project, your available resources and the number of volunteers you have involved. Quite aside from creating a safeguard for your project and helping to provide the best service to your users, being able to show your volunteers that you have thought things through demonstrates in itself the value that you place on their involvement.

Four key questions

1. Why do we want to involve volunteers?

An organisation needs to be clear from the outset about why it wants to involve volunteers in its work. Volunteers should be involved because of the positive benefits to the project, which may include:

● providing better, more flexible, services to users;

- involving and drawing on the skills and expertise of the local community;
- getting closer to the needs of users;
- breaking down barriers between helper and helped.

2. Who will be responsible for co-ordinating the work of our volunteers?

Somebody within the organisation should be responsible for co-ordinating your volunteer programme. Appointing a co-ordinator will help provide consistency and ease communication. Who this is will depend upon the scale of volunteer involvement. It may be a volunteer themselves or a salaried member of staff, but it is essential that everyone knows there is one individual with whom the buck stops on this.

3. How much of our overall budget needs to be set aside for volunteers?

It's a mistake to think that volunteers come free. They do not. They give their time, but there are financial costs involved in any volunteer programme. Money should be set aside for the following:

- *Allowable expenses.* To avoid tax implications, or inadvertently creating an employment relationship, only out-of-pocket expenses should be reimbursed. This will usually cover travel, necessary purchases and may include meals. If a volunteer does not want to claim expenses, suggest that they donate the amount back into the project. This means that you get a clear idea of the amounts involved whether or not individual volunteers choose to claim. This will help you with future budgeting and funding applications.

- *Training.*
- *Administrative costs* – phone, fax, photocopying, stamps, desk space, insurance, administrative backup, etc.
- *Management costs* – the cost of your time and the volunteer co-ordinator's time.

4. What are our volunteers going to do?

Volunteers need to have meaningful tasks with enough to do to sustain their interest and provide fulfilment. It is also important that there is clarity between them and the project/organisation regarding the exact boundaries of their roles and responsibilities so that paid staff (if you have them) do not feel threatened and volunteers do not feel exploited. It is good practice to have written task/role descriptions (see 5.7: Recruiting Staff and 5.9: Employing Staff) and an agreement not to go beyond these parameters without prior discussion.

Recruitment and selection of volunteers

Who will we recruit?

In line with the written task/role description you have come up with, outline any skills, qualities or experience that volunteers will need to fill the role. It is too easy to blindly jump at the first opportunity to take on anybody who shows interest in helping you, and then regret it. Climbing out of a hole is a lot harder than landing yourself in it in the first place. Take care to ensure you get the right person for the right task.

How will we recruit them?

You will need a consistent recruitment procedure that is used for all your volunteers, whether or not they are previously known to the project. This should involve:

- *Making an application.*
- *Attending an informal interview.*
- *Taking up references.* In order to protect your project and the people who use it, best practice means it is always necessary to take up references for all volunteers. This also goes a long way towards safeguarding potential volunteers from being placed in situations they may be unable to handle.
- *Completing a police check.* Where volunteers will be working closely with vulnerable people – children, the elderly, people with mental health problems or a learning disability – police checks may also be necessary (see 5.9: Employing Staff).
- *Feedback.* If it is necessary to turn down an application for any reason, you should always try to give constructive feedback to the person concerned.

Ongoing support

Consistent support, good communication and regular encouragement are the keys to healthy, productive, ongoing relationships with volunteers. Ways to achieve these include:

- Making sure volunteers are regularly updated and therefore aware of any changes taking place within the project that may affect them.

- Giving opportunities to feed back any views to the organisation.

- Creating regular opportunities to participate in decision-making.

- Providing access to relevant training.

- Not making unreasonable demands on volunteers' time.

- Ensuring good working practices regarding holidays and working hours.

- Offering clear supervision/line management.

RESOURCES AND CONTACTS

National Association of Volunteer Bureaux (NAVB)
New Oxford House
16 Waterloo Street
Birmingham B2 5UG
Tel: 0121 633 4555
Website: www.navb.org.uk
Membership organisation for national network of 400 volunteer bureaux.

Local Volunteer Bureau
Contact NAVB above for details, or see local directories, for advice, training and advertising of local volunteering opportunities.

National Centre for Volunteering
Regents Wharf
8 All Saints Street

London N1 9RL
Tel: 020 7520 8900
Website: www.volunteering.org.uk
Range of services to support organisations that involve
volunteers, including information sheets and publications.

Further reading

Essential Volunteer Management by Steve McCurley and
Rick Lynch (Directory of Social Change, 1998).
The Volunteer Recruitment Book by Susan J. Ellis
(Philadelphia: Energize, Inc., 1994).

5.7: Recruiting Staff

Why is your staff recruitment policy important?

1. It is a big decision

Whenever a person makes a decision to start work with you it is a big decision, both for the project/organisation and for the employee. Most people who engage in faith-based community work consider it a serious commitment. Many see it as a significant step in their spiritual journey. It is therefore important that your recruitment policy reflects and respects this depth of commitment.

2. A decision of this kind has a wide impact

When a recruitment decision is made it affects not only the individual and his or her surrounding family and close contacts but also all those who are currently working on the project. Decisions of this kind affect many people's lives. A bad recruitment decision can therefore have wide ramifications and can prove both distressing and time consuming for both the project and the person involved.

3. Recruitment costs time and money

It has been shown repeatedly that poor recruitment policies result in high labour turnover and absenteeism, with a consequent increase in costs. If the right people are recruited in the first place they are likely to stay. If the wrong people are recruited they will either leave voluntarily when they decide to find something that suits them better, or leave unhappily when it is shown that they are not suitable for the job. Time spent in training, managing and ultimately replacing leavers is costly, and the effect on other staff and team morale can be serious.

4. To ensure transparency and consistency

It is an employer's responsibility to ensure that there is no unlawful discrimination in recruitment and selection procedures and that equality of opportunity is an integral part of the process. This means that the employer is obliged to make fair selection and promotion decisions. The way to ensure that this happens is for the employer to commit to clear recruitment and related personnel procedures set out in a written recruitment policy (see 5.8: Equal Opportunities).

Christian employers will want to seek in all areas to place the highest priority on how they treat their people. There is no magic to this – it is simply about putting yourself into the shoes of those working for you and so 'experiencing' your own policies.

People like to know where they are, so be consistent. Develop a recruitment policy and procedure, write it down and then stick to it. Avoid the temptation to dream up new processes as each vacancy arises. Most people will be content if they know what to expect, why they expect it, and how and when it will happen.

5. It is evidence of best practice

If you are seeking statutory funding for your work, you may be required to attach your recruitment policy to any applications for funding.

Forming a recruitment policy

An ideal framework for any community project to work from consists of the following:

1. A recruitment policy statement.
2. Recruitment procedures.
3. A summary of the recruitment process.

1. A recruitment policy statement

A recruitment policy statement outlines your organisation's or project's approach to recruitment. Below is an example policy provided by the YMCA.

Recruitment Policy

The recruitment of people into the YMCA at all levels is a vital activity. It is the first step in the process whereby its principal aims of helping individuals to become whole people can be achieved.

The standards of recruitment practice and the quality of people recruited have a major influence on the image and direction of the YMCA and its capacity to deliver its stated objectives.

The prime aim when recruiting staff is to ensure that the best person is selected for the post.

The selection process for each post in the YMCA is carried out in accordance with the following:

- Procedures recommended by the YMCA, which are efficient, effective and fair and which embody those aspects of legislation which have implications for recruitment.
- Aims and Purposes of the YMCA.
- Equal Opportunities Policy.

It is therefore recognised by the YMCA that all people concerned with the recruitment process must have a clear understanding of the recommended recruitment procedures, the Aims and Purposes of YMCA and the Equal Opportunities Policy.

The Aims and Purposes of the YMCA commit to further the work of Christ in the World. Accordingly, as an Ecumenical Christian Movement, all staff in posts which are central to the fulfilment of the Aims and Purposes of the YMCA are required to demonstrate a clear, personal commitment to the Christian Aims and Purposes.

The YMCA is an equal opportunities employer. The YMCA aims to ensure that no job application is discriminated against on the grounds of sex, marital status, race, colour, nationality, ethnic origin, disability, age or sexual orientation.

2. Recruitment procedures

Your recruitment process from start to finish will be made up of numerous steps:

- *Job description*. The place to start for all vacancies is with the job description. Even if it has already been written for a previous vacancy, it is always helpful to take time to review it. The job description is the basis for the rest of the following process. If your job description is not accurate, it is likely that your selection will be flawed. The job description should define:

  - the main purpose of the job;
  - the role of the job holder;
  - the main tasks to be carried out;
  - the areas and level of responsibility.

  Model job descriptions can be obtained by contacting the Faithworks Consultancy (email: consultancy@faithworks.info; tel: 020 7450 9084). For further information see 6.1: Faithworks Consultancy.

- *Person specification*. This is an assessment of the knowledge, skills and aptitude required to carry out the job description satisfactorily. It describes the requirements of the job in relation to the individual. Broadly speaking there are two parts to this process:

  - The technical ability needed for the job, i.e. the necessary qualifications and experience.
  - The personal qualities required of the post holder.

  It is important that the skills, aptitudes and knowledge included in the person specification relate precisely to the needs of the job. If this is not the case, an employer might limit the number of people who will apply for the job and also, indirectly but unfairly, discriminate against some candidates.

- *Pay and benefits*. Before it is possible to advertise, the question of pay should be considered (see 5.9: Employing Staff).

- *Application forms*. Using application forms is preferable to asking for letters of application or simply relying on questions at interviews. It facilitates comparison, like with like, and therefore helps in the initial sift of candidates. It also provides a basis for the interview and records the candidate's details. More information is available via the Faithworks Consultancy (see 6.1: Faithworks Consultancy).

- *Advertisement*. The aim of any job advertisement is to produce a number of applicants who are able to do the job, while at the same time minimising the number of unsuitable applicants. If you decide not to advertise, you are likely to limit your opportunity for finding the best candidate. The advertisement should include:

- The name of the project.
- Brief information about the project.
- Job title and information about the key tasks, level of responsibility and possible development.
- Essential requirements of the job.
- Hours of work, salary (and other terms and conditions where appropriate).
- Closing date for applications, together with the proposed interview date, if known.
- Name and address to apply to.

If you have not already done so, you need to decide whether you are going to recruit from within your organisation/project or whether you will consider external applicants. (If you are using statutory funds you are likely to be required to advertise externally as well as internally.)

- *Recruitment packs.* Prepare a pack of material that you wish to forward to prospective candidates. This should include the job description and person specification, plus any other relevant information about the project, including perhaps an explanation about how it came into existence.

- *Shortlisting.* Shortlisting is the first stage in a selection process. However, it is also true to say that effective advertising should help people to self-select. The key point about shortlisting is that the process is purely about assessing the candidate according to the information available on the application form. It is not about making any judgement on information supplied on the application form, but simply matching the information available against the required knowledge, experience and qualifications to do the job.

  Ideally a minimum of two members of your selection/interview panel should be involved in shortlisting. Together they should agree which criteria they will use for the shortlisting process and compare results after each has undertaken this process separately. The results should be recorded.

- *Selection.* Depending on the nature of the vacancy, it may be appropriate to use different assessment techniques, in addition to an interview, at the final stage of selection. For some jobs part of the selection criteria may include competent use of machinery, e.g. catering equipment, or the ability to use a computer to draft a letter, compile a balance sheet or give a presentation, etc. In these situations it is helpful to design a simple exercise to test ability. In other jobs the criteria may include the ability to express oneself clearly to others or to work well in group situations. The candidates can be asked to take part in a group discussion exercise with selectors acting as observers.

- *Interviews.* In spite of the limitations of interviewing, it is still the main method by which selection decisions are made. Well-prepared interviews and interviewers can provide essential evidence for good selection.

- *Getting a match.* Whatever method of selection you use, one of the key considerations within the process, apart from finding evidence that the person meets your criteria, is to establish that there is a match between the candidate and the project.

- *Informing candidates of the outcome of the interview.* All candidates should be informed as soon as possible after your decision has been made. Be prepared to debrief the unsuccessful candidates. Given the time and effort most people put into an application, it is good practice to offer to explain why an application was not successful. This will require that you keep a record of the selection process, which you have to hand. Do not attempt to do this without providing evidence of the reason for rejection.

Top tips for interviewing

- Avoid questions that require only a 'yes' or 'no' answer.

- Ask only one question at a time. Rephrase bad questions.

- Avoid long questions, or those that need a long preliminary explanation.

- The best questions are 'When?', 'Which?', 'Who?', 'Where?' and 'Why?'.

- Good questions lead from past answers.

- When you get a lead, follow it by asking subsidiary questions.

- Give your full attention to the candidate and make it obvious you are doing so – they need some form of feedback.

- Listen to the candidate. Do not do all the talking. The ratio should be in favour of the candidate.

- While you want your questions answered in order to collect as much evidence as possible, don't be surprised if you receive unexpected answers. You'll make the candidate nervous if you suggest that this is not the answer you expected. Try suggesting that there may be an alternative response if you think that the candidate has misunderstood the question.

- Never argue or give advice, but give information when this is required.

- Pay attention to what the candidate wants to say, does not want to say and cannot help saying.

- *Conditional offer.* Any offer made to the successful candidate should be subject to satisfactory references and, where appropriate, a satisfactory medical examination or questionnaire. A statement of terms and conditions of employment, detailing salary and job title, should be enclosed (see 5.9: Employing Staff).

- *References.* No offer of employment should ever be confirmed before satisfactory references and other checks, as appropriate, have been received:

  - Wherever possible written references, either from the previous employer or from current voluntary work, should be obtained.
  - References should be checked for factual information, e.g. length of service.
  - If the post applied for involves working with children or young people, the reference request form should always ask for comments on suitability for this type of work.

- *Checks to verify suitability for work with children and young people.* Employers have a statutory duty to carry out certain checks (see 5.9: Employing Staff).
- *Medical checks.* If the job involves physical fitness (e.g. lifting) it is very important to check out the candidate's fitness to do the job before he or she takes it up and suffers illness and absence. To do this you need to tell the candidate that this will be a condition of the job offer and you need to set up the process with a local GP. This may incur a charge. It will also require you to provide the GP with a job description.

3. A summary of the recruitment process

Summarise your recruitment process in a flow chart that

you can then make available to existing staff and candidates for jobs. (See the example in Figure 6.)

Figure 6

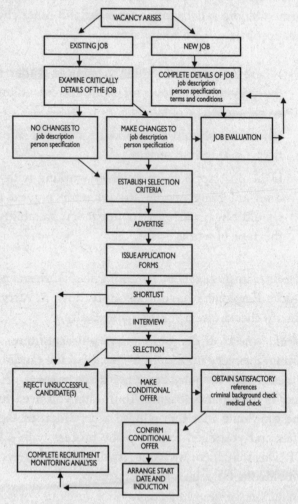

5.8: Equal Opportunities and Recruiting Christians

The concept of equal opportunities is about ensuring that all personnel decisions concerning pay, recruitment, promotion and access to training and development are based solely on an individual's ability to do their job; about using fair procedures to enable you to make fair decisions. It incorporates the principle that all employees should receive equal rights and that rather than ignoring the differences between people in terms of, for example, gender and race, diversity should be recognised and respected.

While every church and Christian organisation would subscribe wholeheartedly to the principles of fairness, justice and equality, most have an issue in terms of their desire to recruit Christians to all, or at least to certain, posts.

The legal position

A statement of your project's policy on equal opportunities, although not a legal requirement, is recommended, including procedures covering recruitment, promotion,

179

transfer, training, dismissal and redundancy. Currently all organisations are obliged by law not to discriminate against employees by reason of their gender, marital status, disability, colour, race, nationality or ethnic or national origins.

If you are seeking statutory funding for your project, you will probably be asked to supply a copy of your equal opportunities policy with your application for funding.

Creating an equal opportunities policy

In order to create a comprehensive equal opportunities policy it is necessary to agree a statement. See the two examples below and note the difference regarding stance related to the issue of recruiting Christians. The YMCA insists on recruiting Christians for only 'posts which are central to the fulfilment' of their goals, whereas Oasis will employ staff in any position who 'are able to carry out their work in a manner which promotes and authenticates the Christian faith'.

OASIS TRUST

EQUAL OPPORTUNITIES POLICY STATEMENT

- Oasis Trust is a Christian organisation committed to social justice and actively opposed to discrimination in society.
- Oasis seeks to provide services on a fair and equitable basis, taking into account only the needs of people referred. No person requiring services from Oasis Trust will be treated less favourably than any other person on the grounds of race, colour, nationality or ethnic origin, gender, disability, sexual orientation, educational status or religion.

- Oasis will seek to employ staff representing all sections of the community it seeks to serve, provided individuals are able to carry out their work in a manner which promotes and authenticates the Christian faith.

As part of its recruitment procedure:

- Oasis will ensure that no job applicant or employee receives less favourable treatment on the grounds of race, colour, nationality or ethnic origin, gender, disability, or is disadvantaged by conditions or requirements which cannot be shown to be justifiable.

- Oasis will consider, seek and use the most effective ways of bringing job vacancies to the attention of persons who may otherwise be disadvantaged (e.g. advertising in the ethnic minorities press, notifying particular job centres, informing particular church networks).

- All job applicants and employees will be asked to complete a form denoting their gender, race and any disabilities. Oasis undertakes that this form will not be made available to anyone involved in recruitment and selection of staff and is for the purpose of monitoring the effectiveness of its equal opportunities policy only.

- Oasis will always welcome appropriate individuals from minority groups among its Trustees and employees and as members of committees advising individual projects.

- Implementation of this policy is the duty and responsibility of all Oasis employees and Trustees. A copy of the policy will be made available to each employee and a copy also given to each job applicant.

- It is the intention of Oasis that no individual or organisation connected with its activities shall hinder the positive implementation of this policy. Any employee may use the grievance procedure to complain about discriminatory conduct. If the matter relates to sexual or racial discrimination or discrimination on the basis of disability then the grievance may be raised directly with the Human Resources Manager. No individual will be penalised for raising such a grievance unless it is proved to be untrue and made in bad faith. Any complaints will be fully investigated in accordance with the procedures as laid out in the Staff Handbook. Any discrimination or harassment proven to have taken place will be regarded as gross misconduct for the purposes of disciplinary procedures.

● Oasis will seek a commitment to equal opportunities on the part of any other agencies, both statutory and voluntary, with which Oasis works in partnership.

YMCA
Equal Opportunity Policy

The Equal Opportunity Policy reflects both Aims and Purposes of the YMCA and the spirit and intentions of legislation which outlaws discrimination. The YMCA will not discriminate or treat any individual less favourably on the grounds of sex, marital status, race, colour, nationality, ethnic origin, disability, age or sexual orientation.

As an employer, the YMCA aims to ensure that no job applicant or staff member receives less favourable treatment on the grounds of sex, marital status, race, colour, nationality, ethnic origin, disability, age or sexual orientation.

The YMCA aims to ensure that people with disabilities are given equal opportunity to enter employment. In doing so, it will fully consider reasonable adjustments to working practices, equipment and premises to ensure that a disabled person is not put at a substantial disadvantage due to their disability. In addition, when staff members become disabled in the course of their employment, every effort will be made through reasonable adjustment, retraining or redeployment to enable them to remain in the employment of YMCA.

Entry to employment and promotion or change of post within YMCA is determined by personal merit and ability relevant to the Aims and Purposes of the YMCA. The Aims and Purposes of the YMCA commit to further the work of Christ in the World. Accordingly, as an Ecumenical Christian Movement, all staff in posts which are central to the fulfilment of the YMCA Aims and Purposes are required to demonstrate a clear commitment to the Christian faith.

It is the responsibility of every individual, both staff and volunteer, to eliminate discrimination by ensuring the practical application of the Equal Opportunities Policy and reporting incidents of discrimination to an appropriate senior member. All allegations of discrimination will be treated seriously. Any discrimination is totally unacceptable to YMCA and anyone found to be discriminating will face disciplinary action.

Sexual and racial harassment are forms of discrimination on the grounds of a person's sex or race. This and any other harassment is totally unacceptable to the YMCA and any such behaviour is considered a disciplinary offence. All allegations of harassment are treated seriously and all practicable steps taken to prevent the behaviour continuing.

Process of implementation

Your equal opportunities policy should be backed up by an agreed process of implementation such as:

- The designation of responsibility for the oversight of the policy.

- The communication of the policy to make it known and understood; the provision of training for all.

- The implementation of procedures to ensure that discrimination, however slight, does not occur.

- The implementation of a procedure for handling complaints of discrimination, including harassment, and ensuring that people are aware of it, how it works and how to use it.

- The collation of statistics and analysis of them in order to monitor the effectiveness of the policy and to determine the nature of any corrective action.

- The use of all the above as part of an ongoing personnel audit.

For more information, contact the Faithworks Consultancy (email: consultancy@faithworks.info; tel: 020 7450 9084). See 6.1 for more information about the Consultancy.

Examples of how to apply equal opportunities to recruitment and promotion procedures

- The job description and person specification for each post should be drawn up and reviewed to eliminate references to non-essential experience or qualifications that might directly or indirectly discriminate against some candidates.

- Job advertisements should be displayed and promoted internally and, where appropriate, externally and be visible to all those who work on the project/in the organisation. They could also be placed in the press.

- The premises used for interview should be easily accessible for disabled candidates.

- Questions about the candidate's personal/family circumstances should not be asked.

- The timing of interviews should be flexible to facilitate family commitments.

- Interviewers should treat each candidate equally and interview them on the basis of the person specification.

- Selection should be conducted solely on the basis of the candidate's relative merits, abilities and qualifications.

- The gender, disability, status, colour, race, nationality or ethnic or national background of the candidates should be monitored by including a detachable questionnaire with the application form.

- Although it is not currently illegal to discriminate against candidates on the basis of their age, it is good practice not to do so, especially as 20 per cent of UK employees are over the age of 50.

Equal opportunities and recruiting Christians

Direct discrimination

Both the Race Relations Act (1979) and Sex Discrimination Act (1975 and 1986) rule that direct discrimination is unlawful per se, unless the employer can show that the discriminatory requirement is justifiable irrespective of the sex, colour, race, nationality or ethnic or national origins of the person to whom it is applied.

So, discrimination on the grounds of sex or race is

unlawful unless there is justifiability. But direct discrimination on the grounds of religion is not unlawful on the basis that there is no current law that makes religious discrimination illegal.

Indirect discrimination

However, the requirement to be a Christian in order to apply for a job may lead to indirect racial discrimination on the basis that a racial group could become disproportionately disadvantaged by imposing this condition.

Indirect racial discrimination occurs when a requirement or condition (in this case being a Christian), although applied equally to persons of all racial groups, is such that a considerably smaller proportion of a particular racial group can comply with it and it cannot be shown to be justifiable on other than racial grounds.

The defence of justifiability

The defence of justifiability is open to any prospective employer accused of indirect discrimination. The key therefore is being able to demonstrate that your recruitment of Christians for all or certain posts is justifiable.

Justifiability is most easily proved by linking the recruitment of all or certain posts with the maintenance and development of the Christian ethos of the work. This is about identifying those posts that are central to the fulfilment of the project's Christian aims and purposes. For example, in a church community centre, it would be justifiable for those responsible for the running of the centre to be Christians in order to ensure that the Christian aims and purposes or the Christian ethos is achieved and maintained. Of course, many churches and Christian agencies would understand that all posts are central to their ethos, aims and purposes.

Justifiability requires definition

The defence of justifiability depends therefore on definition of the organisation's purpose and how the purpose is linked to posts. Once people know what the organisation stands for there is less opportunity for confusion. Vagueness or even reluctance to be clear about the Christian ethos is much less helpful and can appear to be very excluding.

Policy on justifiability

Having thought through the defence of justifiability and identified where you believe it is justifiable to employ Christian staff, it is essential that the policy is written up and agreed by your organisation, project or church.

Justifiability at recruitment

It is essential that employers are clear from the first stage of recruitment (i.e. at the point of advertising) which posts require Christians and which, if any, do not. It is also important that any candidates who are not required to be Christians understand what kind of project/organisation they are joining, what they can expect in terms of the kind of work, what the culture will be like and that their prospects of moving into certain posts may be impeded.

Allegations of discrimination

Allegations of discrimination are unlikely to be made against church staff teams as opposed to church-run services (e.g. a church-run community centre) on the basis that it is easy to see that being a Christian is a genuine occupational qualification for a position as church leader. Therefore care to avoid allegations of discrimination will be required where there are less obvious reasons (to non-Christians) for insisting on having a Christian in the post (e.g. where the project is located away from the church and serving a wider community, and perhaps where a larger team is in place). Care should also be taken in this respect where external advertising takes place and where government funding is in operation.

RESOURCES AND CONTACTS

The Good Employment Guide (NCVO Publications, Regents Wharf, 8 All Saints St, London N1 9RL).

A handbook for small firms (ACAS Publications, ACAS Reader Ltd, PO Box 16, Leicester LE9 8ZZ).

Recruitment Code of Good Practice for Both Recruiters and Applicants (Chartered Institute of Personnel and Development, CIPD House, Camp Rd, London SW19 4UX; www.cipd.co.uk; book sales 01752 202 301; book enquiries 020 8263 3387).

5.9: Employing Staff

Your questions answered about contracts of employment

Who should have a contract of employment?

All employees whose employment lasts for one month or more are entitled to receive a contract of employment. The contract forms the basis of the employment relationship. This is often a difficult area for Christian organisations, where there is an unwritten but nebulous assumption that because we all want to support one another it will therefore not be a problem to accommodate each other's needs. However, because employment is such a classic area for misunderstanding, proper management is essential. Writing down the terms of the contract is a way to minimise disagreements later. An example contract of employment and further details about contracts of employment are available from the Faithworks Consultancy (see 6.1).

What information should be in the contract?

The written contract must cover:

- The names of the employer and the employee.
- The date when the employment (and the period of continuous employment) began.
- Remuneration and the intervals at which it is to be paid.
- Hours of work.
- Holiday entitlement.
- Entitlement to sick leave, including any entitlement to sick pay.
- Pensions and pension schemes.
- The entitlement of employer and employee to notice of termination.
- Job title or a brief job description.
- Where it is not permanent, the period for which the employment is expected to continue or, if it is for a fixed term, the date when it is to end.
- Either the place of work or, if the employee is required or allowed to work in more than one location, an indication of this and of the employer's address.

Where there are no particulars to be given for one of the items required to be covered in the statement (for example, where there is no pension entitlement), this should be indicated.

The contract should also include a note outlining the employer's disciplinary and grievance procedures, and stating whether or not a pensions contracting-out certificate is in force for the employment in question. The disciplinary and grievance procedures do not have to be given within the written statement but can be referred to as a separate document. An employer with fewer than 20 employees is not required to provide these procedures, although the employer must still provide information about how to pursue a grievance (i.e. who to take a grievance to).

When must the contract of employment be given?

It is preferable if the employment contract can be given at the time of confirming employment after the selection. This should be conditional on receiving acceptable references and checks. However, in law all the required terms must be given within two months of the date when the employee's employment began.

What should the rate of pay be?

By comparing the position offered with other similar jobs, or considering local authority rates, you can arrive at the rate of pay. Doing this will give you a 'feel' for the rate of pay and guide you in your decision-making. However, it is not a precise science and if you have more than one job to pay, it is helpful to establish an organisational pay scale.

The overall package you offer can be enhanced by benefits, including provisions like holiday entitlement, occupational sick pay and a contribution to a pension. Remember that recent legislation requires some employers to give employees access to a stakeholder pension and paid holidays. Other benefits can also include flexible working arrangements (e.g. working from home, flexi hours, term-time contracts) and opportunities for training or study leave. Take care to document these arrangements.

Aim at an annual pay review. This is important in order

to keep up with inflation, not just from the employees' point of view, essential though this is, but also from the employer's point of view. Whenever you fail to do this, it makes the increase in future years much harder to bear, as well as making you less attractive as an employer.

Finally, remember that the minimum wage is now in place at a rate of £4.10 for 18s and over.

How should employees be paid?

If the project is already operating PAYE for other staff, a new appointment will cause no problems. However, many churches making a new appointment will not be doing this if clergy salaries are administered by the denomination. In this case, you need to contact the local tax office. Someone will have to take responsibility for handling a fair amount of PAYE paperwork (in Oasis' early years this work was always done by a volunteer). You will be sent various tables for calculating tax and national insurance and will have to account for this on special sheets each month, paying over sums to the Inland Revenue monthly and sending on an annual return.

This work does not necessarily have to be handled by the church treasurer, but it does need attention to detail and keeping up to date with instructions sent by the tax office. Some churches are now choosing to deal with this by using a bureau to handle their PAYE requirements.

It is necessary to provide employees with a written pay statement each time their salary is paid. This must show the gross amount payable, all amounts deducted (tax, national insurance, etc.) and the net amount payable.

Make sure payment is made on time each month (which is normally a few days before the end of the month).

Induction and reviews

The benefits of a process of induction are self-explanatory. It helps the new person to settle in quickly, to know where they fit and who they relate to, and so to feel valued and to operate effectively as part of the team. However, because resources are always limited and the pressures on a project are great, it is the less tangible things like induction that tend to get played down or completely overlooked. A compromised or non-existent induction programme is bound to affect how an employee feels about his or her work and colleagues, which in turn can easily affect their relationship with your clients/users and may eventually even influence whether they stay or not.

Induction tips

- Make arrangements for the new person before the job starts – desk, phone, etc.
- On the first day or so go through the job description. Explain how it fits in with the rest of the work and responsibilities of other team members.
- Introduce the new person to other staff and volunteers. Inform others in advance when the new person is starting.
- Explain the staff/volunteer relationship with the management committee.
- Go through the terms and conditions of employment again. Check that all the pay details (NI/bank) have been forwarded to the right place. Deal with any queries at the beginning.
- Explain where things are, ordering processes, etc.

- Explain the reporting process – who is in charge.
- Explain any rules, particularly health and safety procedures, location of first aid facilities, etc.
- Refer to any rotas – who does them and what is expected of the new person.

Work and personal development review

When people take up the kind of work you have to offer them it represents a serious personal commitment. For them it's a way to work out their faith in their lives. It forms part of their spiritual journey and is therefore an intensely personal matter.

The way in which you, as an employer, respect this level of commitment is all-important. There are a number of positive ways in which you can achieve this. One way is to develop a set of agreed objectives for your employee and then to review them on a regular (annual or bi-annual) basis. This exercise needs to take place between the member of staff and their line manager (i.e. the person responsible for them). You can also enhance this process by offering the employee an opportunity to identify and work on a series of personal development goals, which are then reviewed in the same way. In this way their work can become a tool to develop not only the project, but also themselves.

The ACAS booklet *Employee Appraisal* provides guidelines for setting up this system. (For further information contact the Faithworks Consultancy, details below in 6.1.)

Health and safety

Health and safety at work is covered by extensive legal

requirements. For organisations in the voluntary sector the main piece of legislation is the Health and Safety at Work Act 1974.

As a brief check, the following list contains key legal requirements:

- Write a policy on health and safety.
- Communicate with staff and volunteers about health and safety issues.
- Undertake risk assessments to establish whether any potential work hazards exist.
- Establish a procedure for reporting accidents.
- Obtain a fire certificate.
- Provide first aid equipment and a trained first aider.
- Give employees appropriate training.

The reasonably recent Working Time regulations specify that an employee should not be asked to work excessive hours and should take breaks regularly.

The welfare of children and young people

If the work of your project involves you in the care and welfare of children and young people up to the age of 18, your work falls within the scope of the Children Act 1989.

The Home Office document *Safe from Harm* (1993) was drawn up as a code of practice for safeguarding the welfare of children and young people in voluntary organisations in England and Wales. The following is a summary of the recommendations contained in the code of practice:

- Adopt a policy statement on safeguarding the welfare of children.

- Plan the work of the organisation so as to minimise situations where the abuse of children may occur.

- Introduce a system whereby children may talk with an independent person.

- Apply agreed procedures for protecting children to all paid staff and volunteers.

- Give all paid staff and volunteers clear roles.

- Use supervision as a means of protecting children.

- Treat all would-be paid staff and volunteers as job applicants for any position involving contact with children.

- Obtain at least one reference from a person who has experience of the applicant's paid work or volunteering with children.

- Explore all applicants' experience of working or contact with children in an interview before appointment.

- Find out whether an applicant has any conviction for criminal offences against children.

- Make paid and voluntary appointments conditional on the successful completion of a probationary period.

- Issue guidelines on how to deal with the disclosure or discovery of abuse.

- Train paid staff and volunteers, their line managers or supervisors and policy-makers in the prevention of child abuse.

The Criminal Records Bureau

The Children Act 1989 has given rise to the need for employers to check the suitability of applicants (staff and volunteers) for work with children and young people. The Protection of Children Act 1999 enables identification of those people whose previous conduct, when working with children and young people, demonstrates that they are unsuitable to work with them and then prevents those people from gaining access to children through their work or voluntary service.

To do this the Act makes it a statutory requirement for childcare organisations proposing to offer someone, volunteer or employee, a childcare position to check against the Protection of Children Act list and not to offer a childcare position to anyone who is included on the list.

It is essential for childcare projects to understand how to access this list. (Further details are available from the CRB – see Resources and Contacts below.)

RESOURCES AND CONTACTS

ACAS Reader Ltd
PO Box 16,
Earl Shilton
Leicester LE9 8ZZ
Tel: 01455 852225
Website: www.acas.org.uk

CRB
PO Box 91
Liverpool L69 2UH

CRB info line: 0870 90 90 811
Website: www.crb.gov.uk

DTI Publications Orderline
Tel: 0870 1502 500
Email: dtipubs@eclogistics.co.uk

5.10: Working with National Government

National government is made up of a complex web of politicians, civil servants, chambers, committees, ministries and departments. Together these set a democratic framework within which society operates. This section looks at some of the major opportunities that churches have to work alongside national government in welfare provision in the local community.

(a) THE ROLE OF MPs

Our national government system is formed by the direct election of 659 individual Members of Parliament, each representing a fixed geographical area known as a constituency and each normally having an affiliation to a political party. Every person in the UK, therefore, has an elected representative at the heart of the national political decision-making process, but few of us ever really use our MPs to maximum effect.

What can your MP do for you?

MPs are useful to us on a variety of different fronts:

- They are only too pleased to learn about local constituency issues and take action to see that they are addressed.

- They are keen to hear constituents' views on wider matters of national policy and the impact they are having at a local level.

- They can ensure that your issues or ideas are addressed by the most appropriate minister.

- Most will be members of several parliamentary committees or all party groups and may be able to raise your issues there.

- They can be excellent advocates for particular projects or local initiatives. Their association with your project or initiative will improve its credibility or standing with service users, other agencies and even funders.

Contacting your MP

To find out who your MP is type in your postcode or address to www.whereonearth.com/commons. Alternatively, the Public Information Office of the House of Commons will normally be able to provide relevant information about MPs as well as other matters concerning proceedings in parliament.

You can contact your MP in the following ways.

- Write to them at the House of Commons, London SW1A 0AA.

- Phone the House of Commons' switchboard on 020 7219 3000 and ask to be put through to their office.

- Write to them or phone them at their local constituency office.

Meeting your MP

Nothing beats meeting your MP in person, and he or she will often be quite keen to 'press the flesh' – particularly when there's a potential good news story. The easiest way to meet your MP is to make an appointment or attend a constituency 'surgery'. Normally a constituency office will inform you as to when these will take place, but you can usually expect them to be on a Friday or Saturday, or during a parliamentary recess.

The other way to meet up with your MP is to invite yourself to meet him or her at the Houses of Parliament. Traditionally this is known as 'lobbying' because the place one normally meets is the Central Lobby in between the House of Commons and the House of Lords. This is rather more direct than a constituency surgery and is well worth the experience if you are visiting London or live close enough to travel.

Whatever method you choose to contact your MP, remember that they are busy people. Therefore it is helpful if both letters and conversations are concise and to the point, and that if you want to speak to them in person you give them as much notice as possible.

(b) GOVERNMENT MINISTRIES AND DEPARTMENTS

The Cabinet Office and Social Exclusion Unit

The Cabinet Office aims to co-ordinate and modernise government and is responsible for the much vaunted initiative for 'joined-up thinking'. It does this by supporting the wide variety of ministerial committees established about almost any issue imaginable.

The Cabinet Office currently houses the Social Exclusion Unit (SEU) – a key part of government for developing new ideas and policies aimed at tackling issues of poverty and social exclusion, many of which lie at the heart of church projects and concerns. The Social Exclusion Unit has published a series of important 'Policy Action Team' reports, which are an essential guide to the government direction in addressing social issues. They are helpful as local churches seek to analyse and engage in their own particular contexts. They cover a wide range of issues:

- Jobs
- Skills
- Housing management
- Neighbourhood wardens
- Arts and sport
- Young people
- Community self-help
- Shops
- Anti-social behaviour
- Teenage pregnancies
- Drugs

The SEU was also responsible for developing a national strategy for neighbourhood renewal, the final version of which (the National Strategy Action Plan) contains more than 100 government commitments to tackling poverty and social exclusion in deprived neighbourhoods. All of these reports contain careful analysis and context, which is particularly useful for church community projects in terms of analysing or 'auditing' their local situation, as well as writing funding bids!

Churches would do well to keep informed of the work of the Social Exclusion Unit as it is constantly looking for good examples of how local projects are addressing community needs. Through engaging with government departments in this way, churches can ensure that the benefit of their project can be extended to other areas and different situations.

More details about the Cabinet Office and Social Exclusion Unit can be found at www.cabinet-office.gov.uk/seu.

Other departments

National government is divided into a further 15 to 20 'departments' or functions, each with its own ministerial team led by a secretary of state (a Cabinet member), together with three to six ministers of state or parliamentary under-secretaries of state with more specific briefs.

A full list of departments and ministers is available at www.cabinet-office.gov.uk, but some of the more important departments for church-related work are as follows:

- Department for Culture, Media and Sport (DCMS).
- Department for Education and Skills (DfES).

- Department for Environment, Food and Rural Affairs (DEFRA).

- Department of Health (DoH).

- Home Office (deals with issues such as crime, community safety and immigration, and houses the important Active Community Unit).

- Department for International Development (DfID).

- Department for Trade and Industry (DTI).

- Department for Transport, Local Government and the Regions (DTLR).

- Department for Work and Pensions (DWP) – used to be the Department for Social Security (DSS).

Each department has its own website, where details can be found about the wide variety of work programmes it undertakes. Departments are responsible for developing detailed policies and programmes to ensure the implementation of key legislation. This is often published in the form of guidelines or reports. A number of departments also give grants for particular projects or types of work. For example, the Active Community Unit within the Home Office has a small grants pot for encouraging local community activity.

Information is power! Case study: DTLR

The work done by civil servants in government departments is a valuable source of information for churches and community projects. For example, over the past two years the Department for Transport, Local Government and the Regions (DTLR) has been responsible for developing and

implementing a wide range of new policies and programmes aimed at tackling neighbourhood deprivation.
These have included:

- the New Deal for Communities regeneration programme;
- the development of Local Strategic Partnerships;
- rhe Local Government Act 2000.

The department has provided detailed guidance notes
about how policies are to be implemented. In each case
there has been considerable emphasis placed on the
involvement of local faith communities, which gives us a
clear mandate for action. Knowledge of such guidelines
will prove particularly useful in confronting local authorities and other public agencies that seem unprepared to
adopt new ways of working and are resistant to greater
levels of church community involvement in tackling neighbourhood disadvantage.

The DTLR also houses the Inner Cities Religious Council
(ICRC) and has recently established a Neighbourhood
Renewal Unit, which is intended to be particularly important in ensuring that the faith communities have a greater
role to play in deprived neighbourhoods. It maintains
important statistical information, including the Index of
Local Deprivation 2000 (ILD2000), which combines a wide
range of statistics about all aspects of poverty at a ward
level in order to assess relative levels of deprivation across
the country. This information can be very handy in assessing levels of need in a community (and for filling in funding applications!).

(c) REGIONAL GOVERNMENT

Government Offices for the Regions

National government has an 'outpost' in every English region, as well as in Scotland, Wales and Northern Ireland. The Government Offices for the Regions (GORs) are generally responsible for ensuring the implementation of national policy at the local and regional level. For example, they have been responsible more recently for the implementation and monitoring of area-based regeneration programmes and are now responsible for accrediting Local Strategic Partnerships (see 5.11: Working with Local Government). More information about GORs, and contact details for your nearest office, can be found at www.government-offices.gov.uk.

The second tier of government

GORs do not constitute regional government. This 'second tier' of government in the UK has been recreated since 1997 with the formation of a Scottish Parliament, a Welsh Assembly, a Northern Irish Executive and a series of Regional Development Agencies for each of the nine English regions.

Space prevents a detailed consideration of the new democratic structures established for Scotland, Wales and Northern Ireland, as each has quite different powers and responsibilities, but details can be found at:

- Scottish Parliament: www.scottish.parliament.uk
- National Assembly for Wales: www.wales.gov.uk
- Northern Ireland Executive: www.nics.gov.uk

Regional Development Agencies

In England nine Regional Development Agencies (RDAs) have been established through the passing of a White Paper called *Building Partnerships for Prosperity*. They are:

- East
- North East
- Yorkshire and the Humber
- East Midlands
- North West
- South West
- West Midlands
- South East
- London

The aim of RDAs is:

- to promote sustainable economic development and social and physical regeneration;
- to co-ordinate the work of regional and local partners in areas such as training, investment, regeneration and business support.

RDAs were established by statute as government-sponsored public bodies, with boards that are business-led and which reflect the perspectives and needs of each region and the main interest groups within each region. Their role is to promote greater regional coherence and effective delivery of government programmes. They have significant budgets of their own, and contribute their regional perspective to the work of other central, regional and local programmes and bodies.

An awareness of the work of RDAs is important for churches and community projects, especially as they can often be a source of and/or guide to regional funding priorities – particularly for European funds. Contact information for RDAs can be found at www.local-regions. detr.gov.uk/rda/info.

RDAs are required to take account of the views of voluntary regional chambers intended to bring together elected representatives from local authorities and other regional partners in a forum for the consideration of issues of shared interest, such as transport and land-use planning, and economic development and regeneration.

Church leaders have been involved in the formation of a number of regional chambers. Chambers have been formed in each region, details of which can be found at www.regions.dtlr.gov.uk/chambers/index.htm.

5.11: Working with Local Government

In recent years, local government has undergone some significant changes, largely driven by national government and its desire to improve public services. This section looks at the significance of some of these developments and the opportunities they present to churches and church projects.

(a) LOCAL STRATEGIC PARTNERSHIPS AND COMMUNITY STRATEGIES

One of the most significant developments in local government for many years is the responsibility or 'duty' placed on all local authorities to produce a Community Strategy, addressing the social, economic and environmental well-being of its population. Government has suggested that the mechanism through which this Community Strategy is developed and reviewed should be a new structure called a Local Strategic Partnership (LSP).

Government guidance sets out that the LSPs should bring together the local authority with other public agencies, private sector interests and the voluntary and community sector. The purpose of the LSP is to develop and integrate strategies for addressing the 'well-being' of the community within the local authority area and to set targets for public service provision across five key areas: health, housing, education, employment and crime.

Government guidance also places a heavy emphasis on local community involvement at all levels within the LSP and specifically mentions the central role that faith communities have to play, both at the decision-making table and also in mobilising communities to have their say.

In the 88 most deprived local authority areas, a Neighbourhood Renewal Fund has been established for LSPs to spend on Local Neighbourhood Renewal Strategies. A Community Empowerment Fund, or Community Chest, has also been set aside to establish a Community Network and channel community involvement into the LSP process.

The LSP will be responsible for overall strategy and direction, but part of this will include developing more localised community plans. Once again, churches can play a vital role in gathering local views and opinions about community plans and monitoring them on an ongoing basis. Most local authorities have already established ward or neighbourhood level committees to look at local issues, but these will now need to include much greater levels of community participation and local churches can become catalysts in this process, whether by offering their buildings as meeting places, providing transport or other incentives to local people to take part, or leading small campaigns about particular issues. This means that churches can have an important say in the allocation of the Neighbourhood Renewal Fund across local authority areas.

The inclusive nature of the LSPs means that groups that have often found themselves left on the margins of political decision-making – Christian organisations, churches, other faith communities and ethnic minorities – now have the opportunity, if they are only willing to grasp it, of getting engaged right at the very heart of the policy-making process. And even though political involvement does not automatically guarantee an end to the discrimination so often experienced by faith-based groups when trying to implement new initiatives, it does create a positive foundation to build on. In fact the biggest barrier to local churches engaging in meaningful partnerships to deliver community change is no longer likely to be the 'wickedness' of local councils that exclude Christian organisations, but rather the 'woodenness' of congregations that are too slow to recognise and respond to the opportunities that now exist.

As of April 2001, 71 per cent of authorities had established or were in the process of establishing an LSP, and 23 per cent had plans in place to set one up in the future. To put it simply, for the foreseeable future LSPs are going to be the way in which local welfare initiatives and community development will take place. However, to succeed in this they desperately need the involvement and co-operation of all the key players in any given community, including the churches. Without that buy-in they are doomed to producing huge piles of paper but little else. So the questions each church must ask itself are: Does it consider it is, or wants to become, a key player in the local community? Does it have a significant and unique contribution to make via involvement in an LSP? And ultimately does it believe in a theology of separation or transformation as a way of being God's people?

Government guidance about LSPs and Community Strategies, as well as accreditation criteria, can be found at www.neighbourhood.dtlr.gov.uk.

(b) 'BEST VALUE' AND CONTRACTING OUT

Local authorities are now subject to assessing their services according to the standards of what is known as 'Best Value'. This national government scheme requires local government departments to review their service provision by carrying out a four Cs process:

- Challenge
- Compare
- Consult
- Compete

This has to be done according to a series of performance indicators, or targets.

The 'consultation' process provides an important opportunity for churches and community groups to have their say about how services are provided locally and to suggest alternatives or improvements. A key part of the process is to assess whether or not a private or voluntary agency might be better placed to deliver the service rather than the local authority itself – a process that has led to much contracting out.

Contracting out represents a great opportunity for churches and community projects in that it can give them the chance to provide a local service in a more flexible or user-friendly way. For example, the local authority might contract out its youth work to a church organisation in a particular area. Caution must be exercised, however, that this is not simply an opportunity for the local authority to offload a service on the cheap!

Best Value monitoring in local authorities is undertaken under the watchful eye of the Audit Commission. Should there appear to be irregularities in the manner in which a Best Value Review is undertaken, or in the conclusions it draws, complaints can be made to the appropriate district auditor from the Audit Commission.

Targets and performance indicators again provide a useful source of information for church and community projects, as they measure a wide variety of social and economic factors. Very often statistics are gathered at a neighbourhood or ward level, which can be very useful in assessing where particular areas of need are in a community, or where the local authority might value some support or innovation in trying to tackle a specific problem. In some cases, careful attention to performance indicators over a number of months or years provides important evidence with which to challenge public service providers (see Section 3: Researching Your Community).

More information about Best Value can be found at www.local-regions.dtlr.gov.uk/bestvalue/bvindex.htm and contact details for the Audit Commission can be found at www.audit-commission.gov.uk.

(c) REGENERATION PARTNERSHIPS

Increasingly churches and community groups have been getting involved in area-based regeneration initiatives. Examples range from church leaders chairing regeneration boards, to church buildings receiving large grants to be converted into community centres. In recent years regeneration funding has been made more and more accessible to churches and other voluntary organisations, and despite requiring hours of time and effort such funding can be given in large sums and can seem less arbitrary than applying to the Lottery or grant-making trusts.

There have been successive waves of area-based regeneration initiatives, with national government expecting local authorities to adopt new schemes and approaches to get the new money. However, though local authorities have normally obliged, they have attempted to squeeze such funding into shoring up mainstream service provision in more deprived neighbourhoods rather than adopt new and innovative approaches to tackling poverty and social exclusion as intended. The most recent waves of funding have been the various annual rounds of Single Regeneration Budget (SRB) and New Deal for Communities (NDC) money, which have intensified the pressure on local authorities to ensure that communities – especially the faith communities – play a leading role in decision-making. The government intended that NDC would be community-led, and in many of the 40 or so NDC areas the churches have played a leading role – though often with some tension with the local authority, which perceives it is being usurped.

Recent government announcements mark a switch in policy, which means that new area-based regeneration initiatives will no longer be introduced. Instead they now favour a more strategic approach, which allows Local Strategic Partnerships (see above) to decide where best to spend new regeneration money rather than making deprived areas compete with one another at a national level. But until 2010, when NDC money finally dries up, churches may still benefit from area-based regeneration and, perhaps even more importantly, when all the money is gone and the regeneration agencies move out it will be the churches that are left with the real ongoing task of regenerating lives and livelihoods.

There are countless reports and books about area-based regeneration. Some of the most helpful research has been done by the Joseph Rowntree Foundation (www.jrf.org), but a good starting point for faith communities is *Flourishing Communities*, produced by the Church Urban Fund (www.cuf.org).

(d) LOCAL GOVERNMENT ASSOCIATION BEST PRACTICE GUIDELINES

In February 2002, the Local Government Association (LGA) published *Local Authorities and Faith Communities – A Good Practice Guide*. These are the first ever national guidelines specifically designed to encourage local authorities to work in closer partnership with faith groups.

Faithworks has worked alongside the LGA and other faith groups and local councillors throughout the drafting process of this guide and has requested that the guidelines clearly set out practical tools that will enable local authorities to work proactively with faith communities. Following these consultations, the guidelines include a recommendation that local authorities appoint a faith groups liaison officer to work with groups that wish to develop community initiatives. The document also sets out for local authorities the clear advantages of working with churches well placed to provide sustainable, committed, imaginative and transforming solutions to the needs of Britain's communities.

These are only guidelines, however. The LGA isn't a governing body; it cannot make laws. But it is an influential organisation and the guidelines carry the endorsement of government ministers. The LGA's members – i.e. local authorities in England and Wales – will therefore consider its recommendations seriously. Where local authorities are on the ball they will be proactive in applying this guide, but where they are slower the initiative should be with local churches to ask what progress is being made.

All of this means that much of the initiative is with the churches for the way our communities develop and the extent to which we play a role in that process. Local authorities may be unlikely to start knocking on our door (even with the best will in the world, there are a lot of churches in any one council district), but if we go to them in order to seek Local Strategic Partnerships, if we make them aware of our capabilities, our resources, our enthusiasm, our knowledge and our commitment to the community, it is unlikely that the door will be slammed in our face. The LGA's guidelines have provided all local authorities with clear encouragement and direction to engage more effectively with faith groups and to recognise us as a crucial part of Britain's indispensable voluntary sector. The initiative now lies with us to serve our local community by taking advantage of this fantastic opportunity.

For more information and copies of the Good Practice Guide, contact Nathan Oley, National Co-ordinator of the Faithworks Movement, on 0207 450 9085 or email: politics@faithworks.info.

(e) CONTACTING YOUR LOCAL COUNCIL
AND PUBLIC AGENCIES

Why contact the council?

It was not so long ago that we expected the local council to take responsibility for all the needs of the local community. These days the picture is more complicated. Today we rely on a wide range of public agencies and private companies to make sure that our bins are emptied, our older people are cared for, our young people have something to do in the evenings, our streets are safe, our parks are clean, etc.

Therefore it's important to discover the exact role your local council or public agencies are playing in addressing community needs before going too far in developing ideas for any new community project or scheme:

- If the local council or another public agency is responsible for addressing a particular community need, it would be unwise to unthinkingly duplicate or compete with another service provider.

- If there are problems with the way in which the council or public agency is currently providing a service, there may be an opportunity to share your research and ideas with them to help them provide the service more effectively.

- If you have an idea to address a community need in an altogether different way, the local council or public agency might wish to give advice and encouragement about the added value your plans may bring to existing service provision.

For example, if you were to identify the need for some detached youth work in a particular neighbourhood, contacting the local council to find out about their youth provision may well give rise to a number of crucial pieces of information, such as:

- The council already has detached youth workers working in the area, which the church had been unaware of.
- The council has detached youth workers, but they only work Monday to Thursday, whereas the research shows that they are really needed at weekends.
- The council runs a youth club on Wednesday nights, but has been looking for an organisation that would complement this service with some detached youth work at the weekends.

Such information will have an important impact on any decisions that might be made by the church as to the kind of youth work it might want to carry out and the relationship it will need to build with the local council.

Who does what?

Local councils are still responsible for a wide range of services in our communities, both directly (where council employees actually do the work themselves) or indirectly (where the council pays for another company or organisation to deliver a service on their behalf). And if the local council is not responsible for addressing a particular community need, it is likely that another public agency will be responsible instead. However, every local authority area is different in the way its council and other public agencies divide up and deliver the different services that are supposed to address community needs.

Taking Manchester as an example, the local council is responsible for the following services:

- Adult education services
- Education and schools
- Environmental issues
- Housing
- Libraries
- Leisure services
- Parks
- Planning consent
- Roads and footpaths
- Social services
- Voluntary sector grants
- Waste disposal
- Youth services

A wide range of other public agencies are also involved in addressing community needs. The list below tells you which agencies are responsible for different kinds of services in Manchester:

- Benefits – Benefits Agency.
- Employment – a variety of agencies and initiatives, including Job Centres, New Deal, Action Team for Jobs, etc.

- Learning and skills – Learning & Skills Councils.
- Public transport – passenger transport executives and other agencies.
- Policing – Police and Crime and Disorder Reduction Partnership.
- Fire – Fire Service.
- Healthcare – Hospital Trusts, Primary Care Trusts, Community Health Councils, etc.

Getting in touch

Making contact with the right person in the right department or right public agency can be a frustrating and time-consuming process, but here are five top tips as to how to avoid unnecessary hassles.

1. Start local

Telephoning some distant office and speaking to an anonymous civil servant rarely gets things off to a good start. It is much more fruitful to start local. Local councils have some kind of physical presence in most neighbourhoods, whether a housing office, a local library, a swimming pool or even a detached youth worker! A face-to-face encounter might not achieve immediate results but is more likely to lead to more personal, considered and constructive help – and it immediately starts to build relationships with potentially key local colleagues. A local councillor will probably fall off his or her chair to be confronted by someone with a positive and constructive idea to address a community need at a 'drop-in' or 'surgery', and will no doubt bend over backwards to give assistance and a relevant referral to the right department of the council or a public agency. Health centres, police stations, schools, job centres and other public buildings will all have some idea about who you might need to speak to in addressing a local need.

2. Find the right person

Starting local helps but it is not always the case that local staff are able to address the kinds of issues you need to raise. However, it is vital to discover the appropriate department or agency to deal with your enquiry and which member of staff there has the appropriate role and level of responsibility to give you the information you need.

Your local council will have a leaflet or brochure about the different services it is responsible for and most also have a website. Very often the telephone directory will have a whole page devoted to the local council, divided into the different services it offers. There is also normally a central switchboard number or helpline that will point you in the right direction concerning which department to speak to about a particular issue.

Again, most other public agencies will normally have publicity materials of some sort and increasingly they will have telephone helplines and websites as they try to get more in touch with their 'customers'.

3. Be brief, polite and business-like

Early enquiries, particularly over the phone, need to be brief and to the point. It helps to be very clear as to what are the key pieces of information that need to be shared and what are the questions that need to be addressed. For this reason the person you are calling will probably not appreciate a complete history of your church and a description of each member of the church leadership team (nor will they be immediately interested in the biblical texts that might have motivated this course of action!). When passed from pillar to post on the telephone it is not always easy to remain calm and polite, but it pays to remember that although you might be about to explain your reason for calling for the fifth time in one phone call, it will be the first time the latest person you have been passed to will have heard it. It is not their fault that previous contacts have passed you over to them, and this time it might just be the right person!

4. Arrange a meeting

Where issues you need to address may have longer-term implications or are of particular importance it is often worth arranging a meeting. Face-to-face encounter fosters a much greater level of communication than the telephone and can often lead to more constructive action. In situations where there is the possibility of conflict or tension, a face-to-face encounter forces all parties to treat each other with a greater level of respect and understanding. A meeting can be arranged by telephone, but it is important to be flexible and open about meeting times until a good relationship is built up. It is also worth confirming meetings in writing, particularly with more senior officials or councillors.

5. Keep a record

Whether you are making phone calls or attending a meeting it is always worth keeping a record of who you have spoken to and what has been said and agreed. In the case of phone calls it can sometimes take so long to reach the right person that you forget exactly who has said what by the time you have put the phone down. There is also a danger that busy council staff dealing with many enquiries in a short space of time will forget decisions or commitments they have made. Making a careful note of what has been said, together with the times and dates of conversations, can therefore prove very helpful. On matters of particular importance you should send a copy of any notes to the other party to ensure there is agreement about the decisions reached.

RESOURCES AND CONTACTS

There are various sources of information about local government, but two excellent starting places are:

- The DTLR 'jump-station' – www.local-regions.dtlr.gov.uk
- The Local Government Association – www.lga.gov.uk and www.info4local.gov.uk, which can send you daily emails about important new initiatives for local authorities. This ensures you can always keep up with your council colleagues!

Public Information Office
House of Commons
London SW1A 2DG
Tel: 020 7219 4272
Fax: 020 7219 5839
Email: pio@parliament.uk

Faithworks Consultancy, Membership and Partners

6.1: The Faithworks Consultancy

The Faithworks Consultancy exists to empower and inspire every local church to rediscover its role at the heart of the community by helping you to:

- identify and respond to the real needs of your local community;
- identify and develop existing and potential resources within your church with the aim of using them to meet community needs;
- identify appropriate external partnerships and other resources.

Contact the Faithworks Consultancy if you want more help on:

- how to turn your vision into reality;
- how to accurately assess your community's needs;
- how to identify and develop your church's resources;
- how to develop a successful strategic plan;

- how to build strategic partnerships with local government and other agencies;
- how to access funding sources.

Faithworks Consultancy
The Oasis Centre
115 Southwark Bridge Road
London SE1 0AX
Tel: 020 7450 9084
Email: consultancy@faithworks.info

6.2: Becoming a Faithworks Member

Faithworks membership

Membership of the Faithworks Movement offers you:

- A voice that will be heard in government on issues of social concern and faith in society.
- The opportunity to join together with thousands of other local churches, Christian agencies, projects and individuals to demonstrate visibly that faith works across the UK.
- Access to up-to-date information and support to inspire and equip you in your service of your local community.

Group membership

The Faithworks Movement offers group members (local churches and projects) the following services:

- A free copy of the Faithworks directory of resources.

- Access to the Faithworks consultancy service, offering specialist advice on community action.

- An opportunity to share problems and solutions online for the mutual benefit of those engaged in the same area of community work.

- Advanced booking and discounts on Faithworks training and conferences.

- An opportunity to lobby government more effectively on issues of social concern and faith.

- In-depth access to up-to-date information about funding opportunities and engagement with statutory agencies.

- Regular updates on relevant news, events and resources to help you in your engagement with your local community.

Individual membership

If you believe that faith works, sign up as an individual Faithworks Movement member today. There is no cost involved (though any donations to help us cover our costs will be greatly appreciated).

As a member you will receive the following:

- Regular mailings by email or post, keeping you up to date with the latest developments and news.

- Opportunities to become involved in lobbying campaigns on issues of faith or social concern.

- Opportunities to engage with and be encouraged by others through conferences and events.

- Opportunities to pray in an informed way and stand together on issues that matter.

For more details about group and individual Faithworks membership, or to sign up, visit www.faithworks.info, call 020 7490 9085 or write to:

Faithworks Membership
The Oasis Centre
115 Southwark Bridge Road
London SE1 OAX

6.3: The Faithworks Partners

CARE

CARE aims to serve, inform and equip you, offering people, ideas, information and resources to churches and individuals who are seeking to be 'salt and light' in their communities.

CARE is a charity that runs projects across the UK, making a tangible Christian difference through networks of volunteers. It is active in public life and undertakes practical caring initiatives that affect the lives of thousands.

CARE aims to help you be part of the answer.

Caring

- A hospitality network provides hospitality and refuge, with 350 Christian homes across the UK and a counselling referral service.

- Pregnancy crisis – CARE offers support, advice, information on all options and ongoing practical support, with 150 UK centres.

- Radical care – provides 'forever families', foster care for young people on remand and befriending of adults with learning disabilities.

Campaigning

- CARE campaigns across the UK, in Brussels and the UN on issues of human dignity in family, health, education, politics and media.
- Community involvement – CARE provides training and resourcing for Christians to be more effective light and salt, including over 500 school governors and hundreds participating in grassroots politics.

Communicating

- Getting the word out – CARE helps the church to be informed, active and effective with a Christian worldview and publishes specialist research to inform public debate.
- The next generation – CARE is involved in shaping education policy, getting resources into thousands of schools, speaking to youth about relationships, and facilitating prayer networks for 2,000 schools.

National helplines:

CARELINK – 08457 626 536
linking you to the care you need via a database of 3,000 specialist agencies in 60 categories

CARELINE – 0800 028 2228
providing free, confidential access to advice and counselling on pregnancy and post-abortion care

CHILDLINK – 0845 601 1134
helping those helping children with comprehensive information on childcare issues

CARE – London, Glasgow, Belfast, Cardiff, Brussels

Head office:
53 Romney Street
London SW1P 3RF
Tel: 08453 100 244
Email: mail@care.org.uk
Website: www.care.org.uk
Registered charity no: 1066963

CARE FOR THE FAMILY

Care for the Family's heart is to strengthen family life and to help those who are hurting because of family trauma.

It is their strong belief that prevention is better than cure and that's why they put so much effort into events and seminars for those with already good relationships – to provide quality input so that they can survive the hard times that usually do come along. Most of the programmes are specifically geared to be available to the whole community – not only the faith groups. They are often publicised by churches who see the value of such programmes to the whole of their community contacts. Previous titles include: The Sixty-Minute Marriage, Beating Burnout, Maintaining a Healthy Marriage and The Heart of a Parent.

They also have a number of specific programmes that are delivered at a local community level by those in local churches. The Rapport workshops, Developing Closeness in Marriage and Resolving Everyday Issues, are presented to couples all over the country by trained leaders, often at the request of a 'sponsoring' fellowship. The new training department will provide materials and support for those who wish to run small groups addressing marriage and parenting issues in their local area on behalf of and for any community group they are networked with.

Opportunities for new activity are continually being offered and the next year will see an expansion of their work with single parents, step parents, those maturing in years and those parents who have experienced the bereavement of a child. In all these new initiatives, Care for the Family will be partnering with churches who can help bring support to their local community.

Care for the Family
Registered Office:
Garth House
Leon Avenue
Cardiff CF15 7RG
Tel: 029 2081 1733
Fax: 029 2081 4089
Website: Care.for.the.family@ccf.org.uk

THE CATHOLIC AGENCY FOR SOCIAL CONCERN

The Catholic Agency for Social Concern (CASC) is an umbrella body for Catholic charities in England and Wales.

It seeks to support, empower and co-ordinate those involved in the reduction of poverty and social exclusion in England and Wales; and to ensure that the 'option for the poor' is incarnate in the life of the church. CASC is also part of a wider European and international network of Catholic charities.

There are hundreds of Catholic charities in England and Wales, with a combined annual turnover of over £50m involving approximately 500,000 staff and volunteers who meet the needs of thousands of individuals, families and communities of all faiths and none.

For more information, to donate or participate, please contact:

The Catholic Agency for Social Concern
39 Eccleston Square
London SWIV IBX
Tel: 020 7901 4875

CATHOLIC AGENCY
FOR SOCIAL CONCERN

CHRISTIAN HERALD

As the UK's only interdenominational Christian weekly newspaper, the heartbeat of *Christian Herald* is the local church. Every week, the paper is packed with news of grassroots activity that is making a difference – local churches finding needs to meet, thinking creatively about serving their local community and forging partnerships to improve life for those living around them.

Christian Herald is committed to equipping Christians in a number of ways:

● By helping readers understand the contemporary

issues of the day from a biblical standpoint.

- By telling the stories of local churches that are making their presence felt, day by day, in their villages, towns and cities.
- By stretching readers' thinking – stressing that the gospel has something to say and something to do, no matter what the area of contemporary life.
- By providing the information and challenge that can help stir Christians into life wherever God has placed them: work, home, school, neighbourhood.

Russ Bravo, Editor of *Christian Herald*, says: 'It's our conviction that for a resurgent church to bring the life and love of Christ to a desperately lost world, it must begin to engage with it sacrificially, humbly and passionately. We hope to help in that process.'

Christian Media Centre Ltd
96 Dominion Road
Worthing
West Sussex BN14 8JP
Tel: 01903 821082
Fax: 01903 821081
Website: www.christianherald.org.uk
Registered in England No. 2205345

Christian

CHRISTIANITY+RENEWAL

Christianity+Renewal is a monthly magazine with a readership of over 30,000 who are drawn to its lively mix of news, analysis, columnists, reviews and loads more.

Regular contributors include Tony Campolo, Steve Chalke, Gerald Coates, Jane Collins, Margaret Ellis, Rob Frost, Mark Greene, Joyce Huggett, Jeff Lucas, Mike Pilavachi and Rob Warner.

Christianity+Renewal magazine was launched in 2001 – a merger of two popular and respected titles with their roots in the evangelical and charismatic parts of the church. This 70-plus page magazine aims to reflect its tag line: real life, real faith, in the real world. The readership is drawn from right across the denominations.

The monthly Faithworks feature by Steve Chalke helps readers to put into practice the Faithworks philosophy at ground level. The features help churches and faith-based organisations to identify and focus on key areas to be involved in and equip teams to make the most of the opportunities available. The magazine also carries news stories outlining the substantial improvements in communication between Faithworks and government bodies.

Another regular article, 'Living Churches', features local churches that are making a difference in their community. Articles identify ideas, principles, programmes and initiatives that other churches can learn from and adapt in their own situation.

Christianity+Renewal encompasses news, culture, reviews, persecuted church news, spirituality, biblical strategies, websites to visit, devotions, insight, leadership issues, theological reflection, true-life ministry stories, plus pages of jobs.

The magazine is available from all good Christian bookshops, price £2.50, or through your letterbox by subscription. Save 30 per cent off the cover price by subscribing through direct debit at only £21 for twelve monthly issues.

To subscribe phone 01892 652364, or for more details email monarch@premier.org.uk.

Christianity & Renewal,
Monarch CCP Ltd
PO Box 17911
London SW1E 5ZR
Tel: 020 7316 1450
Fax: 020 7316 1453
Email: monarchccp@premier.org.uk
To sample *Christianity+Renewal* visit our website:
www.christianityandrenewal.com

MOORLANDS COLLEGE

Moorlands College provides a challenging learning environment where men and women, passionate about Jesus Christ, may be nurtured and equipped to impact both the church and the world.

As an evangelical, interdenominational Bible college, Moorlands aims for the highest standards in delivering courses that are biblically based, academically rigorous and culturally relevant, grounding everything in practice to facilitate effective service in today's world, and creating a supportive community which promotes spiritual, personal and relational maturity.

In the past decade or so Moorlands has recognised the crucial nature of understanding what is happening to culture and of building courses that equip students to engage relevantly in community work of all types in a professional and biblically coherent fashion.

The formally agreed Aims and Objectives for two of the

most popular courses, Community and Family Studies and Youth and Community Work, resonate significantly with the Faithworks goals.

For many years Moorlands has educated and trained just a select number of students, who, when they graduate, have the learning, the experience and the skills to work with churches, Christian organisations and local authorities in community development work. Through partnership with Faithworks, Moorlands will now be in a position to share specialist course content and its expertise in training and mentoring with a much wider audience – helping local churches to mobilise their members towards effective community projects.

Moorlands College
Sopley
Christchurch
Dorset BH23 7AT
Tel: 01425 672369
Fax: 01425 674162
Email: Mail@moorlands.ac.uk

OASIS TRUST

Oasis Charitable Trust is an organisation committed to demonstrating the Christian faith in action. It works in communities across the world, seeking to provide holistic solutions to the major social issues of our time. Oasis focuses its activities on the poor and marginalised in society and seeks to equip others to engage in similar work in order to increase the impact of the projects in which it gets involved.

Oasis was founded in 1985 by Steve Chalke. It is organised into four major areas of innovative activity:

- *Community Action* – working housing and healthcare in some of the most vulnerable urban areas, it seeks to teach life skills and to break the cycle of no home, no job.

- *Global Action* – working directly and with partners in 13 countries around the world. Through the exchange of people, expertise and resources it seeks to enable churches and communities to empower some of the world's poorest and most marginalised people.

- *Youth Action* – investing in training tomorrow's church and community leaders. It also runs social inclusion projects across London focusing on those at risk of being excluded from the education system.

- *Church Action* – equipping the church through personnel, training, consultancy and projects. It also develops new models of culturally appropriate expressions of church for the twenty-first century. Oasis Church Action created Faithworks to enable and inspire every local church to rediscover its role at the hub of the community.

For more information about Oasis, please contact:
Steve Chalke
Oasis Trust
The Oasis Centre
115 Southwork Bridge Road
London SE1 0AX
Tel: 020 7450 9000

Fax: 020 7450 9001
Email: enquiries@oasistrust.org
Website: www.oasistrust.org

THE SHAFTESBURY HOUSING GROUP

The Shaftesbury Housing Group is a professional charitable Christian organisation established to meet housing and care needs. As at January 2002 the Group provides homes and/or care services to over 20,000 people, primarily in the South of England.

Shaftesbury Housing was established by the Shaftesbury Society in 1970 and is now a separate organisation. The Group's Parent Association and two of its subsidiaries are Registered Social Landlords, giving access to Housing Corporation funding. The Group has a financial turnover of £60 million and employs approximately 1,400 staff.

The Group has a wide range of experience in relation to housing and care. This includes major urban regeneration, covering commercial development and training opportunities within multicultural communities. Specific examples are the regeneration of 1,000 homes in Hackney and the provision of a community-based housing association for management and improvement of 1,500 homes in Oxfordshire.

The current constituents of the Group are:

- Shaftesbury Housing Association – Parent Association providing family homes and sheltered housing (for rent and leasehold).
- Ashley Homes – residential care and supported housing division.

- Banbury Homes Housing Association (community-based association providing family homes, sheltered housing and some supported housing).

- Kingsmead Homes Ltd – local housing company engaged in urban regeneration, provision of family homes, training and workshop units.

- SOAS Homes Ltd – student housing in London.

- Shaftesbury Student Housing Ltd – student housing and key worker accommodation.

- Cooper Homes & Developments Ltd – development company.

For further information please contact:

Clive Bodley
Commercial Director
Shaftesbury Housing Group
1 Mawle Court
Banbury
Oxon OX16 5BH
Tel: 01295 261669
Fax: 01295 265995
Email: cdb@shaftesburyhousing.org.uk

STEWARDSHIP SERVICES

Stewardship Services is a national Christian charity committed to raising the standard of legal and financial administration in churches and Christian organisations. It provides a range of practical services to help organisations get started as a charity and to meet a number of the ongoing needs and responsibilities that they will face. These include:

Charity formation

Stewardship Services has extensive experience of registering charities and understands the Charity Commission and how to present applications to avoid undue delays. It can set you up with a charitable trust or charitable company specially designed for a church-based charity serving the community.

Payroll administration

Payroll can be a big burden. The service takes care of the details, producing payslips, making payment to the employee's bank account, and dealing with tax and National Insurance.

Employment Contract Pack

Specially designed for use by a Christian charity, the pack contains a model contract of employment, with a number of variations, and helpful guidance notes.

Gift Aid administration

Outsource tax-effective giving to Stewardship Services and enjoy fast and frequent tax recovery and release from the pressure of meeting Inland Revenue requirements.

Accounts examination service

An independent examination of accounts is a legal requirement when income reaches £10,000 pa. Stewardship Services is a specialist in this field. Other services include insurance advice and agency, and stewardship consultancy on communicating vision and fundraising.

Service standards and charges

Stewardship Services aims to provide professional quality at reasonable cost. Contact them for details of charges and discounts to Faithworks members.

Stewardship Services
PO Box 99
Loughton
Essex IG10 3QJ
Tel: 020 8502 5600
Fax: 020 8502 5333
Email: info@stewardshipservices.org
Website: www.stewardshipservices.org
Registered charity no: 234714

YMCA

YMCAs are Christian charities belonging to a national and worldwide movement. They aim to offer young people and their communities opportunities to develop in mind, body and spirit, and so fulfil their potential. Working with people at times of greatest need, they believe in:

- personal and social development – providing life and

job skills training and opportunities for personal growth and challenge;

- nourishing relationships – providing parenting programmes and activities which support young people's transition to adulthood;
- strong communities – providing housing, community activities and sport, health, exercise and fitness programmes.

The YMCA aims to underpin all its work with Christian principles and work for a society where all may flourish. Over 160 YMCAs make up the YMCA movement in England. Each is led by local people for local communities, developing projects to meet identified needs. These local energies are supported by national expertise.

The YMCA, through its local presence, can offer churches and Christian agencies general advice and support based on practical experience in developing and delivering community work and service provision. The YMCA is interested in working in partnership with other organisations that share its ethos and its aims. It has developed standards of best practice for many areas of its work in relation to staff and volunteers, and is willing to discuss how these may be used elsewhere.

YMCA England
640 Forest Road
London E17 3DZ
Tel: 020 8520 5599
Fax: 020 8509 3190
Website: www.ymca.org.uk

SECTION 7:

Signing the Charter

THE FAITHWORKS CHARTER

PRINCIPLES FOR CHURCHES AND LOCAL CHRISTIAN AGENCIES COMMITTED TO EXCELLENCE IN COMMUNITY WORK AND SERVICE PROVISION IN THE UK

Motivated by our Christian faith we commit ourselves to serving others by assuring the following standards in all our community work within twelve months of signing this Charter.

Service to the community

1. To serve and to respect all people regardless of their gender, marital status, race, ethnic origin, religion, age, sexual orientation or physical and mental capability.
2. To acknowledge the freedom of people of all faiths or none both to hold and to express their beliefs and convictions respectfully and freely, within the limits of the UK law.
3. Never to impose our Christian faith or belief on others.
4. To develop partnerships with other churches, voluntary groups, statutory agencies and local government wherever appropriate in order to create an effective, integrated service for our clients avoiding unnecessary duplication of resources.
5. To provide and to publicise regular consultation and reporting forums to client groups and the wider community

regarding the effective development and delivery of our work and our responsiveness to their actual needs.

Clients, staff and volunteers

1. To create an environment where clients, volunteers and employees are encouraged and enabled to realise their potential.
2. To assist our clients, volunteers and employees to take responsibility for their own learning and development, both through formal and informal training opportunities and ongoing assessment.
3. To develop an organisational culture in which individuals learn from any mistakes made and where excellence and innovation are encouraged and rewarded.
4. To promote the value of a balanced, holistic lifestyle as part of each individual's overall personal development.
5. To abide by the requirements of employment law in the UK and to implement best employment practices and procedures designed to maintain our distinctive ethos and values.

Management and outcomes

1. To implement a management structure which fosters and encourages participation by staff at all levels in order to facilitate the fulfilment of the project's goals and visions.
2. To set and to review measurable and timed outcomes annually, and regularly to evaluate and monitor our management structure and output, recognising the need for ongoing organisational flexibility, development and good stewardship of resources.
3. To do all we can to ensure that we are not over-dependent

on any one source of funding.

4. To implement best practice procedures in terms of Health and Safety and Child Protection in order to protect our staff, volunteers and clients.

5. To handle our funding in a transparent and accountable way and to give relevant people from outside our organisation/project reasonable access to our accounts.

Signed on behalf of:

Organisation/Project ....

Denomination (if appropriate) ....

Address ....

....

.... Postcode ....

Minister/Priest/Leader/Project Manager ....

Address ....

....

Email ....

Tel no ....

Signature ....

Date ....

Please photocopy, complete and return to Nathan Oley, Faithworks, The Oasis Centre, 115 Southwark Bridge Road, London SE1 0AX. Alternatively, you can go to the website at www.faithworks.info and sign on line.

Faithworks (Book One)

by Steve Chalke

This informative, provocative book will help clarify the issues and equip us to respond both to human need and to those in government that influence welfare issues and funding.

'Rumours about the church's untimely death have been rumbling around influential places for a long time. The Faithworks Campaign is an exciting opportunity to put such rumours to rest.'

Revd Joel Edwards, General Director, Evangelical Alliance

'The Faithworks Campaign – a message and movement that needs to be heard.'

Revd David Coffey, General Secretary, the Baptist Union

'The Faithworks Campaign is a challenge and an encouragement to local Christians to be intimately involved in their local communities.'

The Rt Revd James Jones, the Bishop of Liverpool

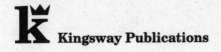 **Kingsway Publications**

Faithworks 2: Stories of Hope

by Steve Chalke and Tom Jackson

Because churches are locally based they respond imaginatively to local needs and issues. No organisation is better placed to deliver the vital practical and spiritual hope which every individual and community needs in order to thrive.

Stories of Hope tells of eight churches from different denominations across the UK who are effectively tackling a wide range of social issues. From debt advice to counselling for domestic violence, from after-school projects to sports clubs, from education to youth work, and from arts initiatives to vocational training – each chapter tells an inspiring story of a local church or individual that has responded to a God-given sense of purpose and direction.

'The stories told in this book are a wonderful inspiration to us all, and speak of the practical hope that the church brings when it is faithful to the call of God. They are an encouragement to us to go and do likewise.'

Sandy Millar
Vicar, Holy Trinity Brompton

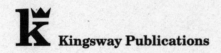 **Kingsway Publications**